BHAVAN'S BOOK U

WITH MALICE TOWARDS NONE

AN AUTOBIOGRAPHY

S. H. BELAVADI

2003

BHARATIYA VIDYA BHAVAN

Kulapati Munshi Marg

Mumbai - 400 007

First Edition, *2003 : 1000 copies*

Price: Rs. 160.00
$ 6.00
£ 4.00

PRINTED IN INDIA by Nilesh Parekh, at Paras Prints,
34, Cowasji Patel Street, 17, Lakhani Terrace, Fort, Mumbai - 400001
and Published by the Bharatiya Vidya Bhavan,
Kulapati Munshi Marg, Mumbai - 400007.
E-mail : brbhavan@bom7.vsnl.net.in
Web-site : http://www.bhavans.info

प्रस्तावना

श्री. बेलवडी यांनी आपल्या जीवनाच्या प्रामुख्याने तीन क्षेत्रातील प्रगतीचा आढावा त्यांच्या या आत्मवृत्तात चपखलपणाने लिहिला आहे. या सर्व क्षेत्रात त्यांच्या व्यक्तीमत्त्वाचा ठसा उमटलेला आहे. कार्यक्षमता, लोकसंग्रह व त्या त्या क्षेत्रातील निपुणता, गुणवत्ता याच्या समन्वयामुळे त्यांची कामगीरी आदरास पात्र झाली आहे. माझा व त्यांचा संबंध वैधानिक कामामुळे आला. १९६२ ते १९७२ या प्रदीर्घ काळात विधानसभेच्या, सभापतीपदाची जबाबदारी चांगल्या प्रकारे पार पाडण्याचा योग मला आला. या दहा वर्षाच्या सभापतीपदाच्या काळात श्री. बेलवडी हे विधान सभेचे तसेच विधान परिषदचेहि सेक्रेटरी म्हणून होते. योगायोगाने त्या काळात विधान परिषदेचे अध्यक्ष म्हणून श्री. वि. स. पागे पदभार सांभाळीत असत. विधान सभेच्या कार्यपद्धतीत विशेष सुधारणा करण्याचा आम्ही यशस्वी प्रयत्न केला. मी, श्री. पागे साहेब आणि श्री. बेलवडी या त्रिवेणी संगमामुळे अनेक सुधारणा आम्ही करू शकलो. संसदीय लोकशाही प्रभावी करण्याच्या दृष्टीने व विधी मंडळाचा दर्जा उंचावण्यासाठी जे खास उपक्रम आम्ही यशस्वी रीतीने पार पाडले त्याचे बरेचसे श्रेय श्री. बेलवडी यांना आहे. शासकीय मंत्र्यांना ज्या सोयी उपलब्ध आहेत. त्या विधान मंडळाच्या अध्यक्षांना उपलब्ध व्हाव्यात व विधान मंडळाची स्वायत्तता सिद्ध व्हावी यासाठी बेलवडी यांना तळमळ असे. तसेच सदस्यांना मानाचे स्थान असावे यासाठी

लोकसभेमध्ये ज्या प्रथा आहेत त्या विधानमंडळात सुरू कराव्यात. या दृष्टीने **'Public Accounts Committee'** चा अध्यक्ष विरोधी पक्षाचा असावा, ही सुधारणा त्याच बरोबर आमदारांनाही थोड्या झुकत्या मापाने अधिकार अधिक प्रमाणात देण्याची प्रथा सुरू करण्यात आम्ही यशस्वी झालो.

संयुक्त महाराष्ट्र झाल्यावर दोन्ही गृहांचे कामकाज मराठीतून चालावे यासाठी आवश्यक ती कार्यवाही व त्यासाठी कायदाही मंजूर करण्यात आला. या घटना मी वानगी दाखल नमूद करीत आहे. सारांश, संसदीय लोकशाहीचा आदर्श विकास व्हावा, यासाठी ज्या विशेष प्रथा कार्यान्वित झाल्या त्यांत श्री. बेलवडी यांचा सहभाग मोलाचा आहे.

श्री. बेलवडी यांचे व्यक्तिमत्व, त्यांची कार्यतत्परता, हजरजबाबीपणा, तल्लख स्मरणशक्ती आणि लोकशाही निष्ठा यामुळे आदरणीय झाले आहे. त्यांचे हायकोर्टातील जीवन कार्य व तेथील कार्यपद्धती, तेथील व्यक्तींची – वकील व न्यायाधीश यांची शैली व कार्य पद्धती, त्याचप्रमाणे त्यांनी वरळीच्या मुक्कामात केलेले सामाजिक कार्य या बाबीही उल्लेखनीय आहेत.

– बाळासाहेब भारदे

माजी अध्यक्ष, विधानसभा

FOREWORD

Shri Belavadi in his brief biographical sketch, has given an account of his life's progress in a forthright manner in the three fields where he worked. In all these fields he has left an impress of his personality in no uncertain manner. His work has earned the respect of all, because of a harmonious combination of his ability, knowledge, merit and public relations in the particular fields where he worked.

I became associated with him because of legislative work.

I had the good fortune of discharging my duties as the presiding officer of the Legislative Assembly in a satisfactory manner, during the long period of 10 years 1962-1972. During all this period, Belavadi was, as the Secretary of the Maharashtra Legislative Assembly was also our Secretary.

Coincidentally, Shri V. S. Page happened to be the Chairman of the Maharashtra Legislative Council at that time. We accomplished successfully, the difficult and delicate work of carrying out special reforms in the Legislative procedures and practices, of both the houses. We were able to bring about several reforms in the field because of the happy combination of joint efforts made by the triumvirate in the shape of myself, Shri Page and Belavadi.

Belavadi, has a lion's share in the difficult task of bringing about the special reforms, needed to strengthen parliamentary democracy and to raise the status of the Lesgilature in public estimation. To ensure the independent status of the Legislative Secretariat and that of its presiding officers and to secure the same facilities and amenities to them, as are available to the Ministers of Government, were matters close to his heart, as was the need to ensure respect and regard for the members of the Legislature. To this end it was necessary to have the same practices and conventions in the Legislature as in vogue in the Indian Parliament.

Thus, it was ensured that the Chairman of Public Account Committee was a member of the opposition in the best tradition of a parliamentary democracy. Similarly, it was seen that the members of the Legislature were treated slightly in a more favourable way.

To ensure that the work of the Legislature was transacted in Marathi following the formation of United Maharashtra, necessary action by way of making legal provisions in that regard and other allied matters was taken. I am mentioning this by way of example. In order to develop parliamentary democracy in an ideal manner and to adopt necessary practices, precedents and procedures required in that behalf. Belavadi's contribution is very valuable. His personality has won due respect from all because of special merit he commanded in the matter of diligence in his work, ready wittedness, sharp memory and faith in democracy.

His life and work in the Bombay High Court, the court procedure, therein the style of functioning of Judges and some of the prominent Advocates of the time, as also his work in the social and educational fields during his stay in Worli after retirement are also worthy of notice.

- Balasaheb Bharade

Ex-Speaker, Legislative Council

PREFACE

The idea of writing my memoirs had never crossed my mind. I had no such intention at any time. I thought it was a matter for the privileged few, who have something worth to say, for the edification of the general public.

But I had wished to write my impressions about the various persons primarily in the Legislature, whom I was able to watch, from my Secretary's table — their style of functioning and their manner of speaking. But I did not know how to set about doing it. Meanwhile, Mrs. Gadre — a friend and resident of our colony, was interested that I should write about the members and the ministers whom I was privileged to observe for nearly two decades. I wished to start doing it, but did not know how.

Then one fine morning, I happened to receive a copy of the book written by my friend — Dr. Keshav Mutalik, former Principal of *Sydenham* College which was, in fact, his own biography.

It had no public interest as such, being principally a personal account of the life of a University Teacher — about his experiences — teaching and learning as he called it; then the idea struck me that I could also try in a similar way. Being in Pune, far removed from my work place — the Council Hall, Mumbai, I have no means to verify the correctness of the various things I have narrated here. I have mainly relied on my memory — and have gone on putting down things as they occurred in my long life. If there are any errors, they are unintentional and due to my faulty memory. For that I wish to be pardoned. I have tried to be as objective and truthful as possible in this narration.

I am grateful to Shri Bala Saheb Bharade — former Speaker of the Maharashtra Legislative Assembly for his excellent foreword, which he agreed to give most heartily.

Thanks are due to Shri V. S. Tamhankar, who prepared the manuscript with great promptitude and efficiency. Last but not the least, to the Bharatiya Vidya Bhavan, a prestigious and world renowned Institution, which so graciously agreed to publish this short narration.

Thanks are also due to Shri Ram Belavadi who spared no pains to arrange for this publication.

– S. H. Belavadi

CONTENTS

BEST WISHES

for

CHRISTMAS AND THE NEW YEAR

from

David Lidderdale

HOUSES OF PARLIAMENT

House of Commons

EMINENT VICTORIANS

In essentials, the House of Commons does not change; but its appearance when in session now is markedly different, in some ways, from its appearance a century ago.

In this picture of a debate in 1860, the Speaker, bewigged, is in his Chair, Government to his right, Opposition to his left; the Clerks sit at the Table before him; the Mace is on its bracket. But the setting—the Chamber destroyed by bombing in 1941—looks richer and more sombre than the quiet, plain modern Chamber. Top hats were worn quite commonly then; there are several in the picture. Nowadays, this hat is seen on Budget Day only, or when a Member raises a point of order during a division, 'seated and covered' (in which case a communal topper is passed hurriedly along to him).

This debate was on the Commercial Treaty with France—a project, initiated by Cobden, which aroused controversy as keen as the modern controversy about Britain and the Common Market. There was much discussion of the effects of this Treaty on the coal and pottery industries and on the import of French wine. Disraeli was quoted as having said that French porcelain was 'so inferior' that it could not be heated, and that the Treaty would mean that 'the dinners of both nations would be improved: England would gain a delightful beverage, and the French (for the first time in their lives) would dine off hot plates'. Nevertheless, Disraeli (seated to the right of the picture) opposed the Treaty strongly.

Palmerston—then, at the age of 75, Prime Minister—is seen speaking for the Government. The aquiline note-taker nearest the onlooker is Sir George Cornwall Lewis, Secretary of State for War. Sitting next to him is Lord John Russell, and beyond (with hands clasped and grey waistcoat) is Gladstone, then Chancellor of the Exchequer.

Far to the left, in shadow, stand Cobden and Bright. The Opposition front-bencher with beard and unkempt hair is Sir Edward Bulwer-Lytton.

The picture was painted by John Phillip, R.A., for Mr. Speaker Denison, whose great-nephew, Colonel W. M. E. Denison, offered it to the present Speaker. It has been on loan to the House since 1960, and hangs in the Members' smoking-room.

Secretaries to the various Legislatures

Assembled in Australia for the C.P.A Conference.

With

The Seasons' Greetings

and

Every Good Wish for the New Year

New South Wales Branch

Parliament House
Sydney

Kindest regards.

Ivor Vidler

In Kolchester with country Council Mayor and Ismail,
the speaker of Ceylon House of Representatives.
When attending a course in British Parliament.

In a procession with the Governor Shree Prakash at the opening of the session.

At the Bombay Airport with Mrs. Belavadi

With the governor Shri Prakash, at a decennial function of the Karnatak Theatres

With Prof. Gokak and his family while felicitating him for the Gyanpeeth award. Mr. Hunshikatti the Chairman of Karnatak Progressive Education Society is looking on.

With Smt. Sujata Manohar a judge of the Supreme Court and Ram Joshi Former Vice Chancellor of the Bombay Univer

At the meeting of the Indian copyright Board in Bombay, with late B. N. Lokur its Chairman.

With S. K. Wankhede, Minister of Finance, V. S. Page, the Chairman of Maharashtra Legislative Council, Shivraj Patil former speaker, Maharashtra Assembly & Lok Sabha, R. S. Gavai, Deputy Chairman of "The Council" and others.

In a group with Mr. Justice Jahagisdar, renowned Surgeon Dr. Baliga, L. M. Patil, Former Minister Maharashtra.

With Ananthsayanam Ayyangar former speaker Lok Sabha, Kanthi former speaker of Karnatak Legislative Assembly, at the Bangalore Conference.

Sri Lanka - temple of the tooth

Belavadi family

With Shree Prakash, Governor of Maharashtra S. L. Silam, Speaker of Maharashtra Legislative Assembly at one of the functions of Maharashtra Legislature

Mrs. Padma Belavadi with late Venutai Chavan wife of Yashwantrao Chavan, Deputy P. M. of India, Smt Prabha Chandrachud, wife of the Former Chief Justice of India and late Smt Sushila Joshi, wife of the Former Cabinet Secretary D. S. Joshi at a function of Mahila Vikas of Bombay.

In a group with A. D. Mani, Editor of Hitawada, Nagpur and Maori lady in New Zealand.

Chapter I

EARLY LIFE — SCHOOLING

I was born in a lower middle class family, at a taluka place Athani in Belgaum district in the erstwhile Bombay Presidency and now the state of Karnataka. Ours was a large family consisting of eight living children – four brothers and four sisters, and two children having died at a very early age. My mother Bharatibai — nee Godubai was the second wife of my father Hanamanthrao. I was the first male child after three sisters before me. The difference in age between me and my father was thus very great and this can be easily seen by the fact that I was studying in IVth standard vernacular – Marathi, when my father retired from Govt. service in the Military Accounts, Pune. The family then moved to Khanapur, a taluka place in the district of Belgaum, about 18 miles from the city of Belgaum. This was in 1918. We had purchased a small house in Khanapur, where we lived for two years. As there were no proper schooling facilities, we had to shift to Shahapur, a place in the erstwhile princely State of Sangli, close to Belgaum city. Thus we established ourselves in Shahapur, mainly for the purpose of education. I was admitted to IInd standard, English, in Chintamanrao High School. I continued my studies there, till I matriculated in 1928.

I was the eldest male member of the family, and I was followed by three brothers in a row — Krishna, Ranga and Ram. They were followed by two more sisters — Kusum and Indu. The family lived in Shahapur and other adjoining places like Vadgaon and Talakwadi — extension of Belgaum. Thus all the members were able to pursue their studies in peace and family security. (see Appendix I)

My father lived a fairly long life but not long enough for our family needs and purposes. My father was drawing a pension of Rs. 45/- p.m. and he worked and added a little extra of Rs. 25/- p.m. or so, to maintain the family fairly well. My father died of old age around 1936 and as Goldsmith observed, he left me a large family of 4 brothers and four sisters but no fortune. This was the common pattern in most lower middle class families. To have a large family, was very common in those days, the concept of small and limited family being relatively modern — a necessity — arising out of limited natural resources. This was so even in European countries, including England and U.S.A. I recollect having read a book by Russell, an American author (for which he got the Pulitzer prize) and if you substitute these American names by Indian ones, it would appear as an Indian family story, instead of the American one, having the same features, such as large family, living jointly, absorbing in the family members both the sick and unemployed.

My earliest recollection starts from a place called Gokak, when I was 4-5 years old. My father was a revenue officer, of the grade of 'Shirstedar' with Magisterial powers. That was a great thing and lent a lot of prestige and power to the position, in a small place like Gokak. It was there that my brother

Krishna was born. I am told he was as precocious and unduly active, as I was quiet and passive though 4 years his senior. It was there that my elder sister Kamalakka, about 10 years old, was married to a boy 16 – year-old Appasaheb, still a high school student, with great pomp and eclat. Appasaheb was the only son of the prosperous lawyer Shriniwasrao Deshpande and we were certainly no match for them. But the offer came from them and my father agreed to it with considerable misgivings and hesitation. Early marriages were quite common in those days. My eldest sister Champakka was married when she was 7 years old. Luckily both the marriages were successful and both lived a long married life. Champakka however succumbed to TB when she was about 40 years of age. There was then no cure for TB. While in service at Gokak, my father opted for deputation to the Military Accounts Department, Pune, so as to earn a little better pension on retirement.

My father came to Pune in 1914/15 and retired from there in 1918/19. It was war time. I was schooling in Bhave School, just in front of Shaniwar Wada. I was in Marathi Std. IV when we left Pune for Khanapur on my father's retirement from Govt. service. While in Pune, I remember that we were living in a small block, in Purandare Wada in Kasba Peth. My father used to walk to his office at Wanwadi, a distance of 4/5 miles and return again on foot. We had a comparatively peaceful and happy life, common to all people of our class.

One or two incidents stand out in my mind during that period. In a petty quarrel with my schoolmates, I had seized the cap of one of the boys. But the boy's father lodged a complaint with the police at Faraskhana and I was in mortal dread of the police for quite some time. It is amusing to see that the father had gone to the length of complaining to the police, in a petty quarrel among boys less than 10 years old. Another instance worth recalling is the dog bite. I was bitten by a dog early morning in our Wada and I was advised to go to Kunnur near Ooty for treatment. The dog had disappeared by accident or design and the Civil Surgeon would not agree for a treatment there, unless the dog was produced. The result was we had to go to Kunnur for a course of injections for a fortnight and while returning to Pune my father took the opportunity of visiting Shree Tirupati for *darshan* of Lord Venkateshwara. I remember to have climbed the 2200 steps in the first stage of the climb and then walked up to the temple, a distance of 7/8 miles. We did that and had *darshan* of Lord Venketeshwara. Later, I continued to visit the shrine every year for many years. During that period, there was an epidemic of influenza when a very large number of people died of it. In our home, only my father and myself were free from it. Others were affected but fortunately, were all cured. The family then moved to Khanapur.

While in Pune, I do not know how Hari Narayan Apte, the doyen of historical novels, happened to visit our place occasionally and partake food with us, which he seemed to relish, specially सार and सांभार of Karnataka. He strongly advised to educate my two elder sisters Champakka and Kamalakka. My mother was very friendly with Maisaheb, the wife of the landlord Dadasaheb, who came from Hubli and knew Kannada. On the whole, we spent a happy life in Pune in congenial surroundings.

How did I spend my life in Khanapur?

I had joined a private school run by one Tinaikar, where I studied a little. The rest of the time, I spent in attending — पुराणाज — religious discourses — which were constantly going on in the temples near our place. I was also fond of attending *Kirtans* which was quite common in those days. This practice I continued even in Shahapur, where there were a row of temples i.e. Lord Venkateshwara, Shri Krishna Murlidhar, Vitthal and Shiva where *Kirtans* were often held. This became a part of my nature and helped to build a religious frame of mind and on the whole, God-fearing, duty conscious, prone to a virtuous life — in short a good character, with a healthy mind in a healthy body.

Khanapur was well-known for its soil, which was suitable for pottery. There was also a tile factory because of easy availability of soil — the necessary raw material. Khanapur also boasted of small manufacturing workshops for कुरमुरे and पोहाज. They were located near the station and were a real speciality.

Khanapur was a small place with no schooling facilities. Life was not expensive and the place was good for people with limited income. Our house, though small, was well-built and was centrally located in Bhat Galli which was at a considerable height from the road down below. Father worked at a place called Mugutkhan Hubli, to augment his meager income to maintain the family. We could have lived happily like this, if studies were not required to be pursued. I was chafing because I had no school to go to and I was in dead earnest to join a proper English medium, recognised school, to prosecute my studies further. I was constantly pestering my father to move out to a place where I could go to school. It was remarkable—

grace of God — that I, a boy of less than 10 years old could crave for studies, when one is inclined at that age, to lead an easy life of fun and play, absence of schooling facilities being good riddance with no blame attaching to me. Through constant and determined efforts, I was able to prevail over father to move out to another place, for continuing my studies. In the process, we wasted about 2 years. Thus, we came to Shahapur, a place near Belgaum, where living was economical, and there were adequate educational facilities for all of us. After a test, I was admitted to IInd std. in English in the Chintamanrao High School in 1922 where I studied in peace happily till I matriculated from that place in 1928.

I spent six years in the school, to reach and pass the Matriculation examination from the University of Bombay. There were no significant events worth mentioning during the period, except that I regularly attended the school, did my studies fairly well and earned the distinction of being recognized as a good and promising scholar. I was a little above 2nd class—but not first class. I was weak in Arithmetic and the result was I missed the prize due to me, because of my failure in the Arithmetic paper. I did quite well in other subjects especially English. Probably I stood first in English in the Matriculation examination in my school.

We had a few good teachers in the school. Shastri taught us Sanskrit and I took a liking for the subject. Because of my interest in the subject, I took a few more lessons in the language, by studying रघुवंश, मेघदूत etc. Gadre, another teacher, very stern in appearance and strict in taking lessons, was good. He seemed to like me. The Headmaster, one Kulkarni, taught us

English and rated me highly in the class. We had genuine respect for our teachers though they punished us mercilessly, if we did anything wrong. On Saturday mornings even if we were late by a few minutes, we were sure of getting punishment — like beating by cane stick.

There was one funny instance, which I must mention here. Father decided to perform my thread ceremony, the beginning of Brahmacharashram — a period of studies. Through inadvertence letters were sent to our relatives, particularly my elder sisters, mentioning a wrong date (तिथि). The date was mentioned as in शुक्लपक्ष bright half of the month — instead of कृष्णपक्ष— the dark half. The result was that nobody attended the ceremony. The relatives landed on the other date as per our letter. Probably we then performed Satyanarayana Pooja and so the whole thing ended as a big joke.

The medium of instruction from IVth std. onwards was English and we had to write our answers in English in all subjects — History, Geography, Science and even Sanskrit. Though I was rated highly in the class, I was no good in extra curricular activities like participating in debates, or making speeches, or taking part in drama etc. I was very shy and that shyness kept company with me throughout my life. In later life, though I had to shoulder some of the things which I shied, I was never comfortable in discharging my role in such matters. If I had not suffered from shyness, perhaps form of inferiority complex, I should have done much better in my career than I actually did.

I was fond of games, and I played kho-kho, atya-patya, langadi, besides cricket, football and hockey. I was second rated in all these but never first rate. The love of sports remained with me all my life. Later in college and afterwards in service, I started playing badminton first, then tennis which I played for 30/40 years. Indeed, I was all for outdoor games including swimming and trekking in forests. I continued to play tennis, till I was 82 years of age. I was fairly good in this and I won a few prizes also in minor matches.

While in Shahapur, I cannot help mentioning an interesting episode relating to cricket. We had two cricket teams, known as Kadabu team from our lane, Acharya Galli and Kodbole team from Saraf Galli. We decided to play a match with the Railway team and accordingly, we requested them for a match. Not knowing much about us and our cricketing talent, they managed to import some very good outside players for playing on their side. The result was disastrous and we were badly beaten, never to be forgotten. Thus ended our cricketing career, abruptly perhaps the world losing a great potential Bradman.

I could manage all subjects with equal ease, whether languages or science or mathematics. Students who were good in languages, did not do so well in mathematics and even some of them failed in that subject. One of my classmates A. V. Kulkarni, was quite good in English and other languages. But he was scared of mathematics. Somehow he managed to pass the matriculation examination but when he joined college and saw that mathematics (Algebra, Trigonometry, Geometry) was compulsory, he took fright and left the college. He joined service in the Postal Department.

In our time, Mathematics and Science were compulsory and students who were not good at these invariably suffered. Now there are number of options and the system is not rigid as it was before. In restrospect, I think, I should have opted for Arts — B.A. and M.A. and not Science.

After preliminary examination in VIIth std., I was permitted to appear for Matriculation of the Bombay University. I had to go to Dharwar for the examination as Belgaum had no centre for the examination. I went to Dharwar along with my friends and stayed in a place belonging to someone known to us. The wells in Dharwar are very deep and we had to draw water from a great depth for bathing. While doing so, the vessel sank in the water below. We had to restore the vessel, which took a great deal of our time and energy. So the morning of the 1st day of the examination was spent in this ridiculous activity, leaving little time for studies. This was no 'hardship' for me, because, generally, I never studied during the actual days of the examination. I used to make my preparations, before and that was quite enough. That suited me. I have never believed in reading at the eleventh hour. Then we went to the examination hall, which was in the Karnataka College, housed in one of the best buildings of the Presidency.

While at Shahapur, during my schooldays i.e. between 1922-28, I must mention a few notable things, which stand out. In 1924 there was an open session of the Indian National Congress in Belgaum, which was, presided over by Mahatma Gandhi. I was in Std. IV then. And I remember to have gone and lived in the camp there as a boy scout. It was then that we had an opportunity to see Pandit Jawaharlal Nehru to whom we presented a guard of honour. Nehru was a handsome young man, with full of promise. Dr.

Hardikar was the head of सेवादल which he had started and it grew from strength to strength under his able leadership. He looked after security arrangements which were superb. He was a strict disciplinarian and built the organization on a sound footing. We were also able to see such national figures as Dr. Annie Besant, C. R. Das and others. The venue of the congress was at a place called Thalakwadi, an extension of Belgaum. There was a well specially constructed to supply water. It had powerful springs and supplied water to the big assembly during that period. The well is still there and is known as the Congress Well.

In 1925-26, the school had arranged a trip to Pune, and other places of interest i.e. Karla Caves, Lohgad, Bhaje Caves and Sinhgad. We went everywhere on foot except for the short train journey from Pune to Malavali, for going to Karla caves and other places. The whole trip may have cost about Rs.10/- But even that was hard to get. I had made a determined effort to join the trip and I was able to do so though with considerable difficulty, mainly because of the expenses involved, small though it was. We also visited Parvati and had Shiva darshan after climbing a long *flight* — of steps.

On the lighter side I have to mention the trick I played on my family, for witnessing dramas of such well-known companies as Lalitkaladars of Bapurao Pendharkar, Balwant Sangeet Mandali, company of Dinanath Mangeshkar-Sarnaik, Hirabai Badodekar etc. I remember to have seen the best dramas during that period like Rakshai Mahatvakansha, Saubhadra, Bhavbandhan etc. I was able to do it because of the low price of the tickets and my habit of sleeping out in the verandah of our house, which was open where one could go out and come in, anytime, without being noticed. The drama used to begin at 10 p.m. at night and I used to go to bed in the verandah after meals, the outside door being closed from inside. I could easily go out and return at about 2 o'clock in the early morning and sleep in my bed in the verandah, without arousing any suspicion.

During Navaratra, there used to be special pooja and other programmes, in the 'Venkatesh Temple' owned by Shahapur Naiks (Shinappa Naik and his progeny). I and Hanamant Naik, (son of Shinappa Naik) used to go to a flower garden in the Thalakwadi extension two miles away and gather 1000 roses every day early morning as per contract. I liked it and did it meticulously without fail. I also used to watch and follow the chariot with the deity installed and witness the Pujas offered by the devotees. I enjoyed all this being of a religious bent of mind.

My father, in his old age, wearing simple clothes, still looking handsome with a very fair complexion, was an epitome of courtesy and kindness. He had retired on a small sum of Rs. 45/- p.m. as pension — but he never complained, never aspired for more, entertained friends and relatives alike though having himself a large family of 7/8 persons. He was scrupulously honest, and maintained cheerful atmosphere at home and outside. He never interfered with us children of whom, he was very proud. He must have been very handsome in his youth, strong and healthy. We children, owe our health, and beauty to our parents. This is a great gift. My mother used to be busy with household chores common in a large family like ours. She was strong and healthy and lived long. Any other woman with so much work, physical and mental, would have collapsed under the weight. I wonder how she alone managed to do all that work.

What friends had I during that time? I had a few friends from Acharya Galli, where we were residing, like Anant Mulgund, Baburao Naik known as Girini Babu because his father owned a flour mill and some members of Naik family with whom I had pretty close relations. Baburao Naik, a colourful fellow, used to visit our place frequently and had good rapport with my father. He had done some schooling but left off later on. He had other qualities, by which he endeared himself to the people. He was quite popular and was good company. Literally he lived on his wits. He was even the President of Shahapur Municipality. He is still living (May he live long). I liked him. Anant Mulgund was another friend, who graduated from Karnataka college, Dharwar and worked as teacher and lived in Hubli, with his wife and children. He was a man of kindly disposition, honest and fair. He was quite intelligent, but never showed off. We were good friends throughout.

I had a good rapport with the Naik family and used to be in their company during Navaratra and Diwali days specially. Theirs was a rich family, being dealers in gold and silver, but they liked us and we liked them, so much so that Shinappa Naik, when he celebrated his only daughter's marriage, Akamma, asked my father to be in-charge of supplies which he gladly accepted. The marriage was performed with great pomp and ceremony. It lasted for full 7 days. There was a marriage procession, with band and other Indian instruments, which would wend its way slowly stopping at intervals when the gathering was regaled with song and dance by well-known dancing girls. We had a good time during that period. Naiks proverbially married into another distinguished family of Potdars from Belgaum. And this was no exception.

I had a lifelong friendship with Hari Narayan Saraf, the only son from a relatively rich family. He had lost his father early in life and he was brought up by his mother, who was also like a mother to me. For me it was a second family. I visited Goa in their company and lived with them for 8/10 days in the temple premises of Mangesh and Shantadurga. We were schoolmates and also college mates in Kolhapur and Baroda. He was much more than a friend. He helped me with money, which I later repaid, and he was, in a sense, instrumental in shaping my career. It was he who prevailed upon me to join the Law College and he even paid fees for the same. I left off M.Sc. studies, and pursued law studies instead. That changed my life altogether. I continued to visit him and his family especially his mother, who was down with paralysis. She was so proud of me that when I became the Secretary of the Legislature — Bombay/ Maharashtra, she took the trouble of coming to the Council Hall and watch me function in the House, from the visitors-gallery. He had three daughters. They were all well married — but one of them died prematurely of cancer. His only son, who was not highly educated, engaged himself in hotel business. My friend Haribhau died quite some years ago. He worked as a medical representative, earned very well and also made some significant donations. May his soul rest in peace.

I was also quite friendly with Bodhrao Naik, Rambhau Ginde and Bhimrao Potdar, who were many years senior to me. Bodhrao Naik was well educated, graduated from Banaras Hindu University. He was a great lover of books and read voraciously. He had to remain in Belgaum, to manage the vast properties of his father-in-law, Bandopant Kulkarni, a rich landlord of Kanbergi — a village near Belgaum. Bandopant had only two daughters and no son. The elder one was married to Bodhrao. He managed the properties very well, effectively and honestly.

I had occasion to appear in an appeal in the High Court, Bombay, as a junior to Jahagirdar, which was filed by a person who claimed to be the natural son of Bandopant Kulkarni. Gangasani, his mother, claimed to be his exclusive mistress. The appeal was dismissed on the grounds that she was not proved to be in exclusive keeping of Bandopant.

The judgment of the lower court, was given by one Kulkarni, a first class sub-judge in Belgaum. He was a very clever judge — but did not enjoy the reputation of being scrupulously honest. His judgment read like a novel. He described the relationship of Bandopatant and Gangasani, as a liaison between a country gentleman and cultured concubine.

Bodhrao and myself remained good friends all along. He helped me a great deal in my early days. Rambhau Ginde was an interesting personality. He always rode a bicycle, though his son, a well-known foreign educated doctor moved in a car. He kept a mistress in a bungalow, some distance away from his bungalow, where he lived with his regular family. He made no secret of this relationship. He had two daughters from his mistress and he even headed the procession openly in the marriage of one of his daughters.

Bhimrao Potdar was a well-known public man connected with a number of public institutions and enjoyed a high reputation. I used to be with them frequently and they liked me. This must have been because of Bodhrao Naik who always treated me kindly. This triumvirate was occasionally joined by Keshav Potdar, who was also my friend. He was a school teacher and retired as the Head Master of Model School, Belgaum. I saw my result in the Matriculation Examination in a local newspaper in the train when we were returning to Belgaum from Athani, my maternal grandfather's place. My sister Kamlakka (Mrs. Deshpande) was with me and I told her about my success in the examination. She was naturally glad to learn this. I still remember my No. (6007) in the matriculation examination. It was my habit to read my result in the next day's newspaper, in all my university examinations. I did not want to trust my friends to wire the results, as I felt any delay or negligence on their part would cause me unnecessary anxiety. It was much safer to wait for another day and see the results published in the next day's newspaper.

Chapter II

HIGHER EDUCATION

Now the important question was how to arrange finance for college education. My father had very limited means and it was not easy for him to finance my college education, besides maintaining a large family. Indeed, he did not want me to study further. Instead, he desired that I should seek a job and augment the family income. This was quite natural from his point of view. He was old and had only his meager pension to run the family. But I had other ideas. I was determined to study further somehow and also lift the family from the difficult situation it was in, in due course. My father had not the patience to wait that long. I had to choose. I opted for a more ambitious course, which was to continue my studies and also take care of the family to the extent possible. Father decided to commute a portion of his pension, Rs. 12/- or so and meet the extra expenses from out of the commuted amount. Thus I was able to join Rajaram College at Kolhapur for the first year. It was the cheapest college at the time. Fees were not very high and living in Kolhapur was comparatively cheap. So the problem was over for the time being.

Father financed my college education for the 1st and 2nd year from out of the commuted pension. He also performed the thread ceremonies of my two younger brothers Krishna and Ranga, at Athani, from the same amount.

In Kolhapur where I joined the college, I had to search for accommodation, as there were no hostel facilities for Brahmins. Every other community had a hostel for its members — such as Saraswats, Prabhus, Lingayats, Marathas, Jains, etc. but none for poor Brahmins. Fortunately, we were able to hire a place — a spacious hall in a building (Latkar's building) just in front of the Mahadwar of Mahalaxmi Temple. There were three other friends with me who were my relatives from Mudhol. We put up a temporary partition in the hall and the two rooms thus available were utilized by us — two in each room. My friends/relatives were comparatively rich and they had joined the college more for enjoyment and fun, than for serious studies. They hardly studied and would not allow me also to study. They used to prepare tea, coffee and cocoa, using the costliest brand. We used to have Upma, Sheera, and other eatables. We had to take our food in a hotel (Khanawal). I took my meals in a Khanawal, near the Mahadwar which was run by a certain person and his wife. His wife used to cook and he used to serve and do other odd things. He took no more than 10/12 boarders and the charges were about Rs. 12/- per month. My schedule was to get ready at 10 a.m., go to the temple and have Mahalaxmi darshan and then go for the meals in the Khanawal. After the meals, I went straight to college, which was near, housed in one of the Maharaja's palaces. I did this for the whole year. We had subjects like English, Mathematics — Trigonometry, Geometry, Algebra — Sanskrit, Science — Physics and Chemistry etc.

The student community consisted mainly of male students; the college nevertheless boasted of a few lady students. My stay at Kolhapur was quite enjoyable. We did boating in Panchaganga river on moonlit nights. My other friends had stint at tennis for some time. Otherwise, we spent our time, eating, chit-chatting and making fun. My friend Haribhau was staying in the Saraswat hostel, where I frequently went.

There was a student by name Ghotage, who was a legendary figure. He was extraordinarily brilliant by all accounts. He used to teach, as a hobby, the students of the hostel, English and Sanskrit. He did not use books. He taught from memory, Meghdoot, Raghuvansh, etc. He was rated very highly in the college and rightly so.

In the intermediate Arts exam. of the Bombay University, there were only two candidates declared in 1st Class of whom Ghotage was one and the other was N. K. Dravid who later qualified for I.C.S. and was my colleague as Law Secretary of the State government. But Ghotage was erratic and whimsical and also prone to mischief. I was there for only one year.

Later on, I learnt that after graduation from Kolhapur, he suddenly disappeared, went to some place in Karnatak, near Gadag, studied medicine and even treated patients. I happened to see him again after a long time in Delhi. When I tried to accost him, he did not like it and wanted perhaps to forget that part of his life. He was later on known as J. P. Naik, was an authority on primary education, and Advisor to the Govt. of India on educational matters. He married Chitra Naik, then holding the position of director of education.

In my life, I have come across only two persons of extraordinary talents. One was Ghotage — J. P. Naik and the other was N. P. Nabar who was an advocate in the High Court, where I had also joined the Bar. Nabar was a good friend of mine — but he drank himself to death. He was excellent in English and Sanskrit. I liked him very much. If he had mended his ways, he could have shone in any field of activity. But his life was cut short. And I lost a good friend.

In the annual college gathering, the students staged a Marathi drama Bhavbandhan by Maharashtra Shakespeare Gadkari and it was a brilliant success. The characters in the drama, like Kammanna, Latika, Dhundiraj and Ghanshyam were portrayed brilliantly— so much so, that it became the talk of the town and there was a request / demand from the palace i.e. Maharaja of Kolhapur, that the drama be staged again specially for the benefit of the Royal family in the Palace theatre. Female characters were played by males as was the practice then. This was done and the students who played the main characters — specially that of 'Latika' became favourites in the palace.

The college had as its professors, such well-known celebrities — as N. S. Phadke, Madhav Julian, Dr. Balkrishna (Principal) with a long tail of degrees, Desai and others. Phadke taught logic and philosophy and not Marathi and Madhav Julian, Persian poetry. We had a very good team of professors and lecturers. In the annual examination (First Year) which used to be college examination in those days, I managed to pass, scoring marks, a little less than required for 2nd class. My other friends — roommates, failed miserably— hardly getting 10 per cent of the marks. Indeed they had already notified their parents as the exam drew near that they could not hope to do much in the exam as it was very stiff. The parents also seemed to agree with that assessment. When they learnt about my result, they were naturally surprised and considered me a genius. Thus ended my first year of the college. My friend Haribhau managed just to scrape through. We were free to return home in early March and the college reopened on 20th June, thus providing for one of the longest vacations. I have always cherished sweet memories of this college life.

The Maharaja of Kolhapur had provided numerous facilities for Maratha students by way of scholarships, freeships, free accommodation in the hostel etc. to enable them to further their studies. I think, Maharshi Karmavir Bhaurao Patil, the founder of the well-known Rayat Shikshan Sanstha, which enabled poor students in rural areas to earn and learn, was a product of Kolhapur. Kolhapur was a pioneer in film production. Master Vinayak — Karnataki, the well-known actor and producer was also the product of Kolhapur college.

For the second year I, and my friend Haribhau and S. V. Garde, my classmate, decided to go to Baroda since Garde's elder brother was studying in Kala Bhavan Technical Institute, and Satish Kalelkar (Kakasaheb Kalelkar's son) who was already studying in Baroda College and who studied with me in Std. VII in the High School at Shahapur, were in a way instrumental in my opting out for Baroda. Thus we, all four from Shahapur, joined the Baroda College. Admissions were easy to get in any college in those days. My father also did not object to my going to Baroda. For accommodation we hired a big palatial place belonging to one Sardar Shinde for a throw-away price — as the place was supposed to be haunted by a ghost. Some servant had committed suicide there and his spirit was believed to be moving around during the night. We along with other friends decided to hire that place, and lived comfortably for the whole year. We occupied spacious rooms on the 1st floor, the ground floor being utilized for cooking. We had hired a cook and managed to run the establishment by rotation. We had a very happy time — arrangements for accommodation and food being excellent for a throw-away price. However, as in Kolhapur, my companions specially Haribhau and Garde, did not themselves study, nor allowed me to study. As a result, for one month I moved to a room in the college hostel and tried to study as much as possible. Both Haribhau and Garde failed in the exam. And Satish Kalelkar left the college and the exam and joined the Dandi (Salt Satyagraha) march by Gandhiji. I had done fairly well in the written exam. In the practical also I had done quite well — but forgetting the time factor, I spent the whole time in doing the experiments and had hardly any time left to write out the results. I heard the warning bell which brought me to my senses and I started furiously writing the results of the experiments performed. It gave me a few minutes for this exercise. But that saved me. By the grace of God, I did not become nervous and with a commendable presence of mind wrote out the answer paper, in that very limited time. I passed the exam in pass class. We all returned to Shahapur. On our way back, we managed to go to a place, called 'Delad' near Surat and had Darshan of Mahatma Gandhi, through the good offices of our friend Satish Kalelkar.

During our stay at Baroda, we visited Sabarmati Ashram in Ahmedabad and managed to join the prayers in early morning, in the Ashram. We also visited the National University (Gujarath Vidyapeeth) of which Kakasaheb Kalelkar was the Vice Chancellor. Satish's previous name was 'Shankar' and he changed it to Satish. He had arranged for this memorable visit. We had a very enjoyable time in Baroda. I had taken my bicycle from Shahapur and I just roamed about. We used to visit Sursagar in the evening for ice-cream and drink excellent hot milk with cream spread over it. The rest of the time we spent in chit-chatting and indulging in fun. We used to visit Kamathi Bagh near the college, where music programmes were held for the public.

We had good professors to teach physics, chemistry and mathematics. I specially remember Prof. Apte, who was well built and was a terror to us. He used to chastise us for being weaklings and advocated eating raw pulses for building strength. He made us bathe with cold water, in the severe cold in winter. He used to say that it was a crime to fall ill in the youthful age. But he was a kindly man and treated us well.

Baroda is a fine city with numerous palaces and gardens. Makarpara palace a few miles away from the city was a superb building with an extensive garden adorned with beautiful statues. There were at least 100 malis (garden assistants) to look after this vast garden. "Laxmivilas' was another palace just near our place. Later, in my life, I was to come in close contact with the persons who had lived there in Makarpura palace. Smt. Nirmala Raje Bhonsale, Ranisaheb of Akkalkot and our minister, was our family friend. She was the granddaughter of Maharaja Sayajirao Gaekwad. Her first cousin Smt Kanchanmala Raje who became Ranisaheb of Nagpur also was our family friend. Her brother Veersing also lived there. He too was our family friend. In Nagpur session, we had to stay there for nearly 2 months and we spent a good deal of spare time together; we had frequent meals at the Bhonsale palace where we were treated in a royal way.

Later I happened to visit Baroda with my wife while returning from the Rajkot conference. I showed her all the places there, especially the 'Shinde Palace' where I lived as a student.

When Nirmala Raje died in her apartment in Akash-Ganga, on Bhulabhai Desai Road, Bombay, I had to attend to her funeral, along with Kanchanmala. She lived a lonely life; Kanchanmala looked after her during her last days, and did obsequies rites with silver I had brought from my place, for the occasion. Mr. and Mrs. Pandit (Kamal Pandit, Padma Lokur's sister) who lived there helped us a great deal in arranging for the funeral.

Baroda was one of few best-administered princely States in India. Maharaja Sayajirao Gaekwad lived for most part of the year abroad — London, Paris, etc. but he always kept a firm grip on the administration of the State. He used to pick up the best candidates for service in his State who competed for I.C.S. but failed to qualify — as the number of seats was quite limited. Thus Jasjit Singh and V. S. Mahajani had joined the Bombay bilingual State, after Baroda merged in it. Aravind Ghose, the Pondicherry Saint, was like the political secretary of the Maharaja, who looked after his correspondence with the Govt. of India. Baroda had tube-wells and had also its own railway. It has one of the best libraries in the country. The subjects, mostly were Gujaratis and for their benefit he got translated all the laws which were in English, into Gujarathi. He was easily the most enlightened and ablest ruler/administrator in the country. Baroda was the first State to merge in the Indian Federation, after India became free. He used to visit his State every year for a month and it was a treat to see the way he was received by the State, and taken to his palace.

I had also an opportunity to see poet Rabindranath Tagore, when he visited our college. He had exceedingly fair complexion, wore a long kurta type apparel, and had long silky flowing beard. He truly looked like a great mythological sage descended from Heaven on earth like Vyas, or Vasishtha. Later in Bombay I had an opportunity to watch a play Tasher desh (Kingdom of cards) with the Poet sitting there singing in his divine voice. He had come to Bombay with his Shantiniketan troupe to collect funds. We had an English Principal S. G. Burrow, and was jokingly known amongst students, as Shankar Ganesh Burrow (शंकर गणेश बरो).

Chapter III

HIGHER EDUCATION (Contd.)

After returning home the thought that worried me was the future. Our limited finances had dried up. Father probably thought that so much college education was enough and I should get myself a suitable job to augment the family income and also shoulder the responsibility of running the house when the time comes. This was quite natural for him to think so. While not disagreeing with him, I thought that I could tackle both these problems partly, primacy being given to my further education. So I decided to utilize the year to earn some money and continue my college education from the next year. But such things are easier said than done. Jobs were hard to get, unless one had the right contacts. I tried to secure a job for some time — but did not succeed.

Instead, I was able to secure a tuition to teach the two children of one Bhattacharya who was then the Executive Engineer, PWD of Bombay. He belonged to the Indian Service in Engineering — ISE — something like ICS. He was an exceedingly nice man. He was very sympathetic and soon I became a member of his family. I learned to play badminton there. He had constructed a special court in the extensive area surrounding the bungalow in the Belgaum fort. It was there that I happened to see D. R. Pradhan, who had just returned to India after being qualified for ICS. He was a bachelor and was accommodated in an out-house, attached to the main bungalow. I was paid Rs. 25/- p.m., which was quite good in those days.

The year went by and I was confronted with the same problem of finding money for further education. I tried to get freeship from the quota of 50 freeships, which the Ruler of Jamakhindi had in S.P. College, Pune because of his handsome donation to the college. I approached my brother-in-law Appasaheb Deshpande, who had some influence in Jamakhindi but he was either reluctant or unable to do anything in the matter. With persistent efforts, I was able to get some money from my two brothers-in-law, Appasaheb and Sheshgiri (the husbands of my two elder sisters) and with that money I went to Pune and joined S. P. College for junior B.Sc. I even approached the Ruler of Jamakhindi direct in his bungalow near Bund-Garden for one of the freeships controlled by him, but I did not succeed.

I lived in a room with a companion in a building called 'Tukaram Ashram' near the college. The building consisted of rooms hired by students like me. Hebbalkar from Shahapur also lived in one of these rooms with his old father. He was a brilliant student but very reserved. One morning his father died and he did not know what to do. He approached me. I gathered a few friends from the college and helped him to take the body to Omkareshwar for cremation. That was my first experience to go to the cremation ground. Otherwise life went merrily with my friends. We used to go to the camp and see English films in West-

End Cinema. My subjects for B.Sc. were mathematics—principal and Physics — subsidiary. I attended college regularly and studied for the exam which was held in Bombay. I passed the exam without much difficulty.

During my stay in Pune, I managed to see some of the best dramas, staged by 'Bal Gandharva' dramatic company. Bal Gandharva, the star performer was at his best and I had the good fortune of seeing him act in these dramas. Today he has become a legendary figure. He completely dominated Marathi stage for well-nigh over 25 years and the theatre — 'Kirloskar Theatre' — was invariably adorned with Poona's drama loving elite as the audience. I used to take my food in 'Badshahi Boarding House' near the college where I used to hear heated political discussions between two socialist stalwarts N. G. Gore and S. M. Joshi, who were also its boarders.

During the Ganapati festival nights, I and my friends, used to roam about in the city and watch the Ganesh mela in every nook and corner of the city. I also listened, with rapt attention, to the music concerts of late Master Krishna, which was a real treat. During the junior year of B. Sc. there was not much pressure of studies and that helped me a great deal to lead a comparatively easy life.

Pandit Hu[illegible]yalkar, a relative of mine, who later became the principal of S. P. College, was with us, though one year junior to me. He was a student of Philosophy. S. H. Kulkarni was another dear friend who used to be with us most of the time. All in all, Poona life was quite enjoyable and I was able to make the most of it, though I had a very limited purse.

For the final year (Senior B. Sc.), I went to Bombay and joined the 'Wilson College' at Chowpatty. I decided to go to Bombay, to earn money, by way of tuitions. My cousin sister, Krishnakka's husband Rangrao Tol, encouraged me to do so, and promised to help me. I landed in Bombay and stayed with them in Popatlal Chawl in Dadar. I did not succeed much in getting tuitions — but somehow I carried on and completed the year. I had taken a room in a newly constructed building near Grant Road and H. V. Imarati was my companion. I used to commute between Dadar and Grant Road twice everyday since I used to take my meals at my cousin sister's place, i.e. Tol's place. Commutation by local train in those days was a pleasure. One could choose any compartment and choose any window-seat. She was a very noble, kindly and affectionate lady, who loved me more than her own brother Ramu. I have always cherished her kindly and loving treatment to me while I lived with them. She was younger than me by about six months. Our relations remained close and affectionate until she died. I would be always indebted to her and her husband, Rangrao Tol, who enabled me to go to Bombay, which opened up exciting possibilities for me. I lived in that great city for nearly 60 years of my life — a fruitful and promising life — which will be dealt with in great detail in due course.

I passed the degree examination (B. Sc.) in 1933 with mathematics as my principal subject and Physics as my subsidiary which I had already passed. I joined for M. Sc. for 'Spectroscopy', a fascinating subject and did some work there. But my destiny led me elsewhere. My friend Haribhau insisted that I should go in for LL. B. so much so that he even paid my fees in the

Law College. As a result, my interest in spectroscopy waned and I gave it up ultimately.

The Law College in those days, was a part-time institution, and the classes used to be held in the mornings and evenings for one period each day, and for two periods on one or two days in a week. I had joined the morning class and used to commute every morning from Dadar, where I was living, to Churchgate and walk up to the Elphinstone College building in the fort area where the classes were held. Students — Parsis mostly staying in the Army and Navy building next to the Elphinstone College building, would request me, when I passed near their building to mark their presence in the Attendance Register. It was rather strange and amusing to tell me so but I did not mind it and obliged them. Most of the students in the Law College worked for a livelihood and attended the college for a degree to better their prospects. I was also working as a teacher in an English School founded by Prof. R. K.Shirodkar, who was my professor of Physics in Rajaram College of Kolhapur. He was a good hearted person and immediately appointed me as a teacher in his school. He was truly devoted and dedicated to education. He even appointed Garde, my friend, as a part-time teacher at my instance who was then studying in the Grant Medical College.

The results used to be very stiff, hardly 20% for the freshers: but I was able to pass the exam in second class (there was no pass class (III). It required 50% marks in the aggregate. I continued for second year LL. B.; leading the same kind of life. I had joined the evening class this time. We had a good team of professors. Dr. Ambedkar was the Principal of the

College and he taught us Constitutional Law. He was an excellent teacher and I entirely relied on the notes, which I made after his lecture. I used to study in the Elphinstone College Library by borrowing the books there. I had no books of my own. I passed the second LL.B. exam in October 1935 in second class. I had joined the Law College in October 1933. It is pertinent to observe that I did not take leave from the school where I was teaching, for preparation, except during the actual days of examination. We answered two papers of 3 hours' duration everyday, for 3 days.

During this time, I was living with my friends Bhandiwad and others in Tarabaug Estate in Girgaon. I was giving tuitions and working from early morning till evening. In the afternoon, I went to the Elphinstone College Library to study. In the evenings I was free to spend time with my companions. We had a companion — a Gujarathi person — Tansukhbhai Bhat — living with us. He was extremely well-behaved, disciplined, soft-spoken, leading a well regulated life. He had spent years in Sabarmati Ashram under Mahatmaji's care and discipline and was in regular correspondence with Gandhiji. During vacations, he used to spend his days in Gandhiji's Ashram. Gandhiji used to look after him and even financed him when he went out. He was an interesting person. Another friend Melligatti (original) but known as Puranik having been given in adoption to his maternal uncle, came to live in the Estate as our neighbour. He was married to Indutai also a close relative of his, living there with his maternal uncle. It was a love-marriage, probably against the wishes of his uncle Puranik, who did not like such things, being possibly an orthodox person of the old world. He had retired as the Head-master of prestigious Govt. Sardar High School in

Belgaum and had no issues of his own. Hence my friend's adoption.

He was a strict disciplinarian and obviously did not like things like love-marriage taking place under his own roof. So the couple ran away to Bombay, and lived in our building. Both were extremely likable persons, and we all together formed a happy group. We always called him Melligatti: his original name. Both were forward looking and modern in outlook and took part in Kannada dramas, which were staged. He was a graduate — B.A. and had also passed an Accountancy examination — which later on came to be recognized as equivalent to C.A. — Chartered Accountant. He was a very witty person, who regaled us with his witty remarks. Later he entered Govt. Service in the Sales Tax dept. and retired as Dy. Commissioner of Sales Tax. They were also my next door neighbours in the Foreshore Bungalow near Cuffe Parade in Bombay. They were extremely religious, studied scripture together, spent the life after retirement in the sacred place called 'Swadi' in Karwar district of Karnataka. He died very recently, which was a shock to me. I met his wife, who lived in Pune with one of her sons. She bore her sorrow for her departed husband in a manner, fitted for a spiritual person that she is. May his soul rest in peace.

In the meanwhile, in May 1936, I married Padmavati— younger daughter of late Bodhrao Kadkol, who had died prematurely of cancer, while serving as Ist Class sub-judge at Bijapur. The marriage was celebrated in the Maruti temple premises of Nuggikeri in the outskirts of Dharwad. Padmavati was living with her uncle Shridharrao Kadkol, who was then a Farm Superintendent in a govt. Farm near Dharwad. The collector of Bijapur who was the custodian of

Kadkol's property as a court of wards, sanctioned the necessary amount Rs. 5,000/- for the marriage after satisfying himself that it was a proper proposal in all respects after verifying the same from Padmavati, the bride and her escort, a cousin, lawyer Pralhadrao, at Bijapur. Padmavati was a bold girl and she answered all questions satisfactorily put to her, by the collector concerning the proposal. It was she, who at the age of 15 years, when her father died, approached the collector for taking over the property for safe custody and maintenance, as a court of wards, after getting it safely locked and sealed, to the utter disbelief and consternation of her maternal uncle, who had rushed there on receiving the news of the death.

Bodhrao had only one son — her stepbrother, a minor of 10 years of age. But for the promptitude and swiftness of action the property could not have been saved and the same would have been frittered away by her maternal uncles. She, no doubt, incurred the wrath and hostility of the relatives on her step-mother's side. Padmavati had a stepmother, who was the second wife of Bodhrao. But their relations were cordial and affectionate and there were absolutely no ill-feelings of any kind between them.

But the situation quickly changed with the death of Bodhrao. Her stepmother, though basically of good nature, was prone to be misled by her own scheming brothers. But she also died of cancer after a few months. The relations between the two families however remained strained and hostile. My wife Padmavati though living with her paternal uncle in the farm continued her vigil and used to meet her brother off and on, on the sly to satisfy herself that he was doing well. Thus the relations between the brother and sister remained close, cordial and affectionate throughout because of her genuine interest in the welfare of the boy.

I was not rated very highly in the matrimonial market of those days as I had nothing by way of property like lands and house but, on the contrary was saddled with a large family to be brought up after the death of my father, who was already quite old. I agreed to the marriage considering all the circumstances, which was performed in a simple manner without any unnecessary expenditure. I had passed Ist LL.B. exam and was studying for second LL.B. We spent very little for my own purposes as a bridegroom and diverted portion of it for the benefit of my brothers and sisters, who were quite young. Rao Bahadur Koimottur, who had retired as the collector of Belgaum and in whose family, my wife Padmavati was a constant fixture, had a very good opinion about her and strongly recommended her to me. My wife's aunt was the daughter of Rao Bahadur and my wife spent the weekends in the Rao Bahadur's house during her stay at the farm. Rao Bahadur's words were prophetic and she proved to be not only what he had predicted but much more. She brought life and light in our family and encouraged me to prosecute my studies and even start my legal practice in the Bombay High Court. She was an extremely talented person and was possessed of rare courage and confidence. She carved out for herself a permanent honourable position in our family, loved and admired both by the young and the old.

After passing my LL.B. exam I decided to join the High Court Bar on the appellate side and try my luck and luck indeed helped me a great deal. My father was not that ambitious and desired me to take up a job or practice in Belgaum, and so lighten his burden to some extent. But I did not share this view and continued with my ambitious plan in Bombay. As a result, I could not give him any immediate relief in the way he wanted, to my eternal shame. But it proved to be a profitable gamble, for the general benefit of the family. I did well at the Bar, though quite a junior and was able to help the family, by way of proper maintenance and education of brothers and sisters. My brother-in-law Appasaheb (Kamlakka's husband) was from the very beginning indifferent and did not seem to think much of us. But with my passing of LL.B. exam everything changed and he started whole heartedly not only to support me in the legal practice at the bar but also to respect me and our family generally. He helped me a great deal by way of building up practice at the Bar. He even specially engaged me to argue a revenue case before the Dy. Collector Shirhatti in Belgaum, the opposite side being represented by barrister S. A. Desai of the Bombay Bar. I think, we won the case.

Chapter IV

LEGAL PRACTICE & HIGH COURT SERVICE

I started my legal practice at the Bar, with no means or help, in a big city like Bombay, literally relying on God's grace and luck. Nor had I the assured support from the family like father, uncle or brother and others, none of whom, were lawyers, who could support me by way of building up legal practice. Generally, only such persons who came from the lawyers' families in the districts dared to practice in the High Court, on the Appellate side, where the practice consisted solely in the shape of appeals and applications against the decisions of the lower Courts in both civil and criminal cases in the districts. For this, one required assured support from the lawyers in the districts.

The High Court at Bombay has mainly two sides, the Original side and the Appellate side. On the original side, the Court heard cases arising in the city of Bombay, while on the civil side the cases had higher pecuniary claims — higher than that permitted for the small causes court, and on the criminal side, sessions cases of crimes triable by sessions courts. At that time, City Civil and Sessions Court had not come into being.

On the original side only those who had passed the original side examination or who were called to the Bar in England could practise. There was then a system called the dual system which required the assistance of solicitors who would prepare the case, act for the clients and render help to the Counsel, who would only present the case and argue in the court. O.S. examination was made deliberately stiff, so that it became the monopoly of a few persons. The system was borrowed from England which suited the English Barristers, who practised in Bombay, aided by solicitors' firms, which were also English. Even today the firms carry English names like, Little & Co., Crawford & Baylee — though the personnel now is entirely Indian. Such a system was in vogue only in Bombay and Calcutta, where perhaps such a system was needed to deal with highly complicated cases involving huge claims with efficiency.

In course of time the system was abolished, in its original form and it permitted Advocates to appear on any side provided the practice prevailing on that side was followed, that is to say that on the original side, the advocate had to be assisted by a solicitor — no such thing being required on the Appellate side. In my time however the dual system was in full force. The two sides were like watertight compartments: the original side had such legal luminaries as Sir Jamshedji Kanga, C. K. Daftari, Motilal Setalwad, Bhulabhai Desai and others. The Appellate side had stalwarts like A. G. Desai, H. V. Gumaste, R. A. Jahagirdar, D. A. Tuljapurkar, P. V. Kane and others. Coyaji and Govindlal Thakore though technically of the original side always appeared on the Appellate side as counsel. They had practically monopolised the side. But it suited junior advocates like me, who could always engage them in big cases.

I started my practice in right earnest. I remembered the advice of K. M. Munshi, who told me to be in dead-earnest about my work and advised me to remain in the High Court till it rose for the day, whether I had work or not. I was teaching the son and daughter of Munshi at the time. So to gain experience and know-how of the legal practice, I joined the chambers of R. A. Jahagirdar and started reading there. I used to go there in the morning and return home in time for the meals and proceed to the High Court well before it resumed its work. I used to carefully attend to the cases which were being heard in the several courts and thus I gained insight into the working of the system. I used to listen to the arguments of senior advocates and Counsel, and mark their way of presentation of facts and marshalling of arguments on facts and Law in the case. I greatly benefited by them. By right contacts and personal efforts I was able to gather sizable practice, though quite a junior at the Bar. I was considered to be one of the promising Advocates at the time. My contemporaries and friends at the Bar i.e. M. G. Chitale, V. S. Desai and D. V. Patel — were raised to the Bench in due course of time. But my destiny led me elsewhere.

I was invited to become the Dy. Registrar of the High Court on the Appellate side by the new Chief Justice Sir Leonard Stone. I was really meant for the Registrar's post — equivalent to that of a District Judge, but was asked to serve as a Dy. Registrar to gain experience. I was 35/36 years of age at that time and it was a tempting offer, made to me in the most flattering terms. I readily accepted the offer without even enquiring about the salary of the post because of the persuasive manner in which it was offered and also because of my heavy responsibilities towards the family. My friends however did not like my accepting the offer. There were others at the Bar who envied me for my luck. One senior Advocate Choksey, who subsequently became the Govt. Pleader in Gujarat High Court, told me that luck had visited me at midnight by knocking at my doors arousing me from my sleep and offering this gift to me on a platter. Any way, to this day, I have not regretted my accepting the post and did my work in the new position, believing in the dictum of Geeta, which said that whatever you do, do it well. Apart from this, the job opened up other opportunities to which a reference will be made in due course.

Thus ended my practice at the Bar, which was hardly of 9 years' duration. When I was appointed as a Dy. Registrar of the High Court, under Sir Leonard Stone, the Chief Justice, Mr. Justice Lokur arranged a dinner at his place 'Bolieu' on Malabar Hill and did me a great honour by inviting me to join the dinner. It was a small group which included 2/3 judges of the High Court. I was a young junior officer in the august company of High Court judges. I cannot forget this gesture shown to me, by a great man, which he was.

What was my experience at the Bar, short though it was? The kind of work transacted on the Appellate side of the High Court consisted of Appeals and applications, civil and criminal, against the decisions of the lower courts. There were First Appeals, which were filed against the decisions of first class sub-judges, who enjoyed unlimited pecuniary jurisdiction in civil suits filed in their courts. Appeals in such cases lay directly to the High Court. Second appeals were appeals against the decisions of the District Courts, in Appeals filed before them against the decisions of second class sub-judges, who had limited pecuniary jurisdiction.

In execution matters also, there used to be first appeals and second appeals. There were applications in revision which invoked the revisional jurisdiction of the High Court, which was wide but very much restricted by case-law. Then there were appeals against the orders under the Civil Procedure Court, called A.Os. There could be letters-patent appeals against the decisions of a High Court Judge sitting singly. But he had to certify that the case was fit to be heard by a Division Bench consisting of two judges.

On the criminal side there were appeals against the decisions of the Sessions Court and also applications for revision invoking the revisional jurisdiction of the High Court under Cr. P. C. Then there were what were called confirmation-cases, which came up before the High Court for confirmation of death sentences passed by the Sessions Court in murder cases. The Law required that the death sentence passed by the Session Court must be confirmed by the High Court.

These came automatically, whether one appealed or not. The record of proceedings viz. evidence as noted down by Sessions' Judge used to be printed and the whole thing came before the High Court in the shape of paper books, on the basis of which cases were conducted. There were, of course, records of proceedings in the original regional languages like Marathi, Kannada and Gujarati, which were the real records of the cases, which could be referred to for verification if any doubt arose in any respect, while dealing with the matter on the basis of paper books, which consisted of English notes made by the Sessions judges. The arguments could be on both facts and law.

The High Court decisions constituted the case-law embodied in the law reports. This was binding on the lower courts. The Chief Justice, under the rules,

Constituted Benches, as they were called i.e. Single Judge Benches, Division Benches consisting of two judges and a full Bench of 3 or more judges to hear and deal with complicated questions of law especially when there were contradictory decisions of the Division Benches on the same questions. When the two judges differed, the matter used to be referred to a third judge, named by the Chief Justice and his decision was final in the matter.

On Mondays and the following days, one Division Bench heard criminal cases, appeals, applications including confirmation cases, till all the cases of the week were heard and disposed off. In my time, Chief Justice, Sir John Beaumont and another judge heard all the criminal cases of the week. They used to finish the work in 2 or 3 days and then take up other work.

A case used to be ready for hearing when the record was complete, parties served and other formalities completed. There used to be what was called a Ready List — which was the earliest list of cases ready for hearing. The cases then moved on to the tri-weekly and then to the weekly lists and finally to the daily list. From this one could know the progress of the cases coming up for hearing. These lists were notified as and when ready. Senior lawyers could manage early or later hearing of the cases to suit their convenience. This, more often than not, resulted in injustice to the junior lawyers, who were helpless. Sir John Beaumont, the Chief Justice (1930-1942), did not take much interest in administration. But this was all changed by Sir Leonard, which left little scope for manoeuvre.

Sir Leonard was however a good administrator. He was a very strict judge, keen to do justice. Morarka, a mill-owner from Sholapur was convicted and sentenced to one month's imprisonment, for an economic offence. But he was evading to go to prison on grounds of his health and managed to enter a nursing home instead. The news flashed in this connection, attracted the attention of the Chief Justice Sir Leonard Stone, who was holidaying in Mahabaleshwar, during May vacation. He directed me on the phone to call for the case-papers and arrange a sitting of the Bench and for the hearing of the case. Accordingly the case was put up before the Bench, presided by him and the hearing fixed. At the hearing, he directed constitution of a panel of doctors, to examine Morarka and report on the state of his health and whether his health permitted him to go to jail and suffer the imprisonment. The panel of doctors unanimously opined that there was no such danger and he could be safely sent to jail. I, as the Deputy Registrar, utilized the services of the Sheriff of Bombay — the first of its kind in the history of the High Court, — to see that Morarka was duly conveyed to jail and the compliance report sent to the Chief Justice. Sometimes unwanted publicity results in such developments.

Sir John was a great judge. He used to sit like a statue with rapt attention when the Advocate opened the case and intervened only later when he had doubts on facts or law. The Advocate for Appellant opened the case followed by the respondent's Advocate, if called upon, by the Court and in that case followed by Appellant's Advocate again by way of reply. After this the Court would dictate the judgment in the open Court. Only rarely in complicated cases, the judgements used to be reserved to be delivered later on. All the records of the cases to be heard, used to be sent to the concerned judges on the previous day, so that the judges could come prepared for the hearing.

In this way the cases were quickly decided. On admission days which was Friday, the Judge sitting singly used to admit or dismiss the case after hearing the Advocate, depending on its merits. The judges did strenuous work for full five hours everyday, from 11 A.M. to 2 P.M. and 2.45 p.m. to 4.45 p.m. The Courts did not work on Saturdays and Sundays. The Courts started working exactly at the stroke of 11 a.m., without a minute's delay. Before that, the judges used to gather in the Judges Corridor for a few minutes, before they entered their respective Courts at the appointed time.

The Chief Justice and the two Administrative Judges, used to dispose off administrative matters between 10.30 a.m. and 11.00 a.m. in the mornings and again after 4.45 p.m., if necessary. But this was rare. Mr. Justice Macklin, used to say jocularly that he was prepared to waste public time rather than private time, after the Court rose for the day. There used to be two Administrative Judges, one for the Appellate side and the other for the Original side, to assist the Chief Justice in administrative matters. Generally the Administrative judge on the Appellate side was from I.C.S. Cadre because of his administrative experience. This was the standard pattern until independence (15th August 1947). Sir Leonard Stone, who succeeded Sir John Beaumont as Chief Justice retired prematurely as India became independent. Sir Leonard Stone was succeeded by Mr. Justice M. C. Chagla, superseding Mr. Justice K. C. Sen, who belonged to the I.C.S. Cadre.

Sen felt very much hurt by this appointment, especially as he was due to retire in less than a year. He never joined other judges for lunch during the lunch-hour, as was the practice and remained confined to his chamber. He was not rated very highly as a judge, but some amends were made to him for this injustice by appointing him as the president of the Industrial Tribunal where he worked for some years more. I knew him fairly well. He was a kindly man with a good heart, and most *unostentatious* in his behaviour.

So for the first time in the history of the High Court, a non I.C.S. Judge — Mr. Justice Gajendragadkar was appointed as an administrative judge with no background of any administrative experience. Mr. Justice Bawdekar, I.C.S. had been appointed as an Administrative Judge by Chagla, but it was changed and Gajendragadkar came to be appointed in his place. Generally no judge was anxious to do this administrative work in addition to his usual judicial work and such appointments were considered innocuous. But with Mr. Justice Gajendragadkar's appointment the position changed. The judge seemed to acquire rare importance, probably because of patronage and prestige in the districts. Later Mr. Justice Lokur said to me casually and half jocularly that Gajendragadkar would continue as an Administrative Judge as long as he remained in the High Court. And so it was.

I have given here broadly the position in the High Court and the way it functioned, on the Appellate side under the laws then in force. Cases came to us for filing appeals or applications or to represent the other side, in appeals etc. filed by others.

In the very early days of my professional career, Mr. Justice Sen who was doing admission work on a Friday, dismissed the appeal I had hoped to get admitted. I was naturally upset, since it was one of the few matters entrusted to me. When I met Mr. Justice Sen at his residence later, he remembered the case and said that he was sorry to have dismissed it. It is possible that he dismissed it because, he knew me so that no charge of favoritism could attach to him, psychologically speaking or he may have been quite right in dismissing it for aught I know. Anyway this is how I felt about it. For a junior, cases came to him few and far between and a dismissal like this would affect his future career. But Judges — especially drawn from I.C.S. Cadre can have no idea of this. In another case, which was a criminal appeal in a dacoity with murder case, the accused were sentenced to transportation for life. The matter came up before a Bench consisting of Mr. Justice Divetia and Mr. Justice Rajadhyaksha. I argued it as well as I could but the judges were not convinced and they decided to call for the original records and stood the case over. When the record came and the matter put up again for hearing for admission, I argued with some heat and vehemence — but of no avail. They refused to admit it. I went down to the Bar-room still in a state of anger and despair.

Really speaking such matters should be admitted as a matter of course, without much argument, because, the accused were entitled to have the case looked into afresh, at least once, as they had been heavily sentenced. Bansilal Thakore, an Advocate and son of Govindlal Thakore, eminent counsel, told me that his father who had his case next after mine, did me justice by thundering, when confronted in his case, which was an application for revision where the scope was limited. "I have seen, My Lords, how appeals are treated in this Court", suggesting that the dismissal of the appeal, (referring to my case), was totally wrong. M. M. P. V. Kane, an Advocate at the Bar, who later on became Bharatratna, the highest title in the land, observed that I was wrong in losing my temper like that and that I should be more careful in future. In the evening I happened to meet Govindlal Thakore on Marine Drive and he complimented me for the way I argued that case. I decided in my mind to follow Govindlal, who was such a great success at the Bar rather than Kane, though a great Sanskrit scholar, had not done so well at the Bar. There were several other cases in the course of my practice, some I argued myself while in others I had the assistance of senior counsel — where I had a mixed bag of success and failure. All in all, I did fairly well at the Bar.

Another case where I had the cheek to argue, against my opponent M. M. P. V. Kane in a case of Hindu Law, involving the interpretation of सौदायिक and non सौदायिक property. Kane was challenging the decision of a division bench of the Court in the matter and wanted the case referred to a full Bench, for a proper and correct decision based on the correct interpretation of the terms in the original text. The arguments lasted for quite some time and the Court reserved the judgement for delivery at a later date. Kane was very hopeful for a favourable verdict. But it seems that due to the lapse of time, the judges forgot the arguments and adopted the safe course of confirming the decision of the Division Bench and I had the credit of winning the case.

I must mention here a few other cases with which I was not directly concerned — but have a general interest. One Jahagirdar, a Lawyer practising both at Bijapur and Indi, a taluka place, had the habit of opening letters from Indi, inserting fresh contents in the letter and redirecting it to Indi, without affixing postage stamps. This had gone on for years, but one fine morning, he was caught red-handed while doing so, since his clerk, who had fallen out from him after a quarrel helped the postal authorities to arrest the letter in question and start prosecution against Jahagirdar. The Magistrate however acquitted him for reasons best known to him. It had become the talk of the town creating suspicion in the matter. Govt. appealed against the acquittal. R. A. Jahagirdar, who was then the govt. pleader in the High Court transferred the case to his assistant B. G. Rao because the accused bore the name of Jahagirdar and probably was a relative of his. Since the case had created much public criticism, Rao thought it safer to engage the Advocate-General to argue the case. Jahagirdar, the accused then, as a proper match, engaged Bhulabhai Desai, an eminent counsel at the Bar, to defend him. Bhulabhai Desai used to tell his client to be ready for a sentence of two years, which he thought the Court would impose. When the case came up for hearing, Bhulabhai Desai made a suggestion to the Court that he would advise his client to plead 'guilty' provided the Govt. agreed to impose a lighter sentence or fine. The Advocate-General asked for time to consult the Govt. When the case came up for hearing again, the Advocate-General said that Govt. desired the case to go on and be decided on merit. They did not agree to the terms. The case went on for a whole day and strangely enough, the Court confirmed the acquittal given by the lower Court. This speaks volumes for the legal talent and nice subtle arguments made by Desai in the case.

In a criminal case from Dharwar district (Karnataka State), two persons were burnt alive in broad day-light in a certain village probably because of some village feud. The number of accused involved was around 50. There were rumours that the Police In-charge of investigation had been heavily bribed and so was the position right up to the Session's Court in the long chain of proceedings preceding it. The result naturally was acquittal of all the accused. The Govt. filed an appeal against acquittal and the appeal was conducted by the Advocate-General Motilal Setalwad, on the Govt. side and Bhulabhai Desai for the accused, — the respondents. There was a printed record of 2000 pages. Chundrigar Advocate then practising in the High Court who subsequently became P.M. of Pakistan, had been engaged to defend the accused in the Session's Court presided by Miabhoy. It seems that rumours of heavy bribing had reached the High Court and scales appeared to be tilted against the respondents — accused. Bhulabhai had been constrained to observe in the course of hearing that he was already in possession of a verdict in his favour and he should be treated as such. After long and strenuous arguments, the Court reversed the order of acquittal and sentenced the accused to various terms of imprisonment. But none of them was sentenced to death as might have been the case. This was due entirely to Bhulabhai's great forensic skill in handling the case. He had a photographic memory and he could say which witness had said what at a moment's notice. The strangest thing was that there were absolutely no markings on his paper books.

There was an interesting case from Belgaum, a civil suit, where the claim for a share in the property was based on the position that the claimant plaintiff, was the natural son of one Bandopant Kulkarni, a rich landlord — his mother being in his exclusive keeping. This was refuted by the other side and they had evidence to show that it was not so and several people used to visit the mother during that time. It was rumoured that the 1st class Sub-Judge who heard the case, had been bribed by both sides and each side expected a verdict in its favour. Meanwhile the judge had a paralytic stroke and the case went before his successor. The judgement was kept ready sealed in an envelope. The new judge asked the parties whether he could open the envelope and deliver the judgement or they wanted a trial denovo. As each side was hopeful of a verdict in its favour, they readily agreed for the delivery of the judgement, which was kept ready. The verdict was against the plaintiff, who had filed the appeal in the High Court subsequently. I knew the parties — the landlord's side — and I happened to be engaged as a junior to R. A. Jahagirdar. I think, the case was actually argued by Motilal Setalwad, who had been engaged as a counsel. We won the case. My engagement was more or less, as a help to me, the landlord's representatives, being my friends. It was an interesting case and the lower Court Judge, had written a good judgement, reading like a novel, using expressions like 'the country gentleman' and the cultured concubine to describe the liaison between the two.

In a criminal revisional application, before the Chief Justice Sir John Beaumont, the arguments advanced by Govindlal Thakore were marked by a rare display of courage, frankness and aggression. Thakore appeared for the respondents and the case did not seem to involve any point of law which alone could justify the intervention of the High Court. But somehow the Chief Justice was inclined to intervene against the settled case-law. This was how it went.

Thakore: "My Lord, there are 12 reported cases on the question. I have appeared in all these 12 cases.

I have argued in 6 of these for the proposition and against the preposition, in the remaining six. In all these cases the decision was the same and now it was too late for Your Lordship to lay down any novel proposition of law and interfere in a matter like the one in question, which involved no point of law. The decisions were all by the Division Benches and they are binding on Your Lordship". The Chief Justice was upset and angered by this onslaught and he interfered in the case and reversed the verdict. But later on this was set right which was the correct thing to do.

The High Court was adorned with a galaxy of legal luminaries. Mention may be made of Bhulabhai Desai, C. K. Daftari, Motilal Setalwad, Jamshedji Kanga, Coltman, K. M. Munshi, H. C. Coyajee, G. N. Thakore from the original side, and A. G. Desai, R. A. Jahagirdar, H. B. Gumaste, P. B. Gajendragadkar, J. C. Shah from the Appellate side, among others.

Bhulabhai was very sharp, persuasive, with a photographic memory, always keeping an eye on how the judge's mind was working and making arguments accordingly. He was very respectful to the Court, and argued his case most convincingly. C. K. Daftari's opening of the case was something like a treat. It opened like a novel. He was felicitous in his expression having spent years in England for his education, was full of wit and humour and would just make his point in law, by reading the section in the text in his inimitable way, emphasizing word or words in the section to draw out the intended meaning. Motilal Setalwad, with a handsome personality, with silvery hair, gold rimmed glasses, was an embodiment of dignity and decorum. He was very meticulous in his work, never did any slipshod work, and did full justice to the case. He was extremely fair in his dealings and never over charged any client. Both Motilal Setalwad and C. K. Daftari adorned the position of Advocate General in the State and Attorney General/Solicitor General at the Centre in Delhi.

Bhulabhai was an important political figure and the nation would always remember him for the way he conducted the case on behalf of I.N.A. in Red Fort, New Delhi and the tremendous efforts he put in for days on end to prepare the case and argue it most convincingly. Jamshedji Kanga with a very impressive personality walked like a colossus in the corridors of the High Court, making it difficult for youngsters like me to keep pace with him.

In one case, I remember, where he made the arguments by Govindlal Thakore look ridiculous. He wore a Parsee Pagadi on his immaculate European dress and looked very impressive with his large natural build. His chambers provided the training ground for youngsters under his stewardship and produced a string of eminent Advocates like Seervai, Palkhiwala and Andhyarjuna and others. This is a good example for others to emulate. F. J. Coltman, an English Barrister, was very brief in his arguments and would dispose off a large number of cases cited by the opponent, by just pointing out how they did not apply to the case in question.

K. M. Munshi was a colourful personality whom I knew well — but had no opportunity to see him function in the Court. He spent much of his time in politics. He was a highly cultured person with great literary attainments to his credit. He would be always remembered for building up Bharatiya Vidya Bhavan—an institution known all over the world for the great work it did and is doing in making India's ancient culture and traditions familiar to the whole world.

H. C. Coyajee, who always appeared on the appellate side as counsel, was in great demand and was in many ways quite the opposite of Govindlal Thakore. He was exceedingly persuasive in his arguments, greatly respected the Court and would call Court's decree or order, as his Lordship's command. He practised for more than 60 years at the Bar and was highly respected by all. He was soft and suave in his manners and conduct. Govindlal Thakore was curt and aggressive in Court and would often seem to snatch a judgement in his favour from the reluctant judges by dint of sheer advocacy on facts and law. He had the Case-Law at his fingertips. He argued with great force and vehemence and displayed rare courage and fearlessness.

A. G. Desai, the doyen on the appellate side, was a keen lawyer, persuasive and persistent. He was a bit tricky and shifty in his arguments. But he knew where he was leading. On the whole a very able and successful lawyer. He had his fixed place in the Bar-room, where he used to be surrounded by litigants and mofussil lawyers alike. He argued all his cases himself. I have never seen him engaging any counsel from O.S.

H. B. Gumaste was a senior lawyer from Karnataka. He had amassed a large practice. He would sometimes engage a senior counsel from O. S. like Coyajee, Thakore, if the client so desired. He was a very generous man and very hospitable. On Fridays, when the Courts adjourned for the week-end, we juniors used to follow him while going home, in Tram No. 8 and he used to buy tickets for all of us. Then we all got down and went to his place in 'Maharaja Building', near Majestic Cinema, in Girgaum. We usually used to have *upma* and tea served before we went to our respective places. He was the first advocate from the Appellate side to have constructed a huge building in Fort area, calls 'Dhannur', named after his native village. He was a man of considerable property in Bombay and Poona. He mixed with us freely, was least ostentatious as were most Advocates from the appellate side. We liked him.

R. A. Jahagirdar was another senior Advocate from Karnataka. He was very systematic in his work and commanded a good chunk of cases from Karnataka. His expression was not so polished — but he was solid in his preparation of the case both on law and facts and made his plea difficult to resist. I was his junior. He treated me well and we had excellent rapport and relations. When Gajendragadkar asked him if I would work as his junior, he just observed that a person working as a junior to an Advocate for long would always be recognized as such. He mentioned the cases of Madbhavi, a junior to Desai and Durg from Dharwar a junior to Dixit, who though senior and quite able in their own right were in public estimation only juniors attached to seniors. I took his advice and never thought about the matter a second time. Gajendragadkar was probably annoyed at my reluctance to join him. He did not seem to forget it when he was raised to the Bench and appointed as an Administrative Judge to assist Chief Justice Chagla. I happened to be appointed as a Dy. Registrar, in which position I had to remain for a much longer time than I had expected. At any rate, this was my feeling at the time.

Gajendragadkar was another senior Advocate from Maharashtra, who had gathered a large amount of practice at the Bar, was very felicitous in his expression and argued his cases impressively. In course of time he was raised to the Bench and in due course he became a Judge of the Supreme Court and also its Chief Justice. His judgement in the reference case between U. P. Legislative Assembly and the U. P. High Court judges (Allahabad) in the matter of privilege and contempt showed his misgiving about the Legislature, and being an opinion matter in a reference case was not treated as good law, and was never followed by the legislative bodies. He was an erudite scholar and was well-versed in Sanskrit. After retirement he did some valuable work in Bharatiya Vidya Bhavan.

J. C. Shah was another Advocate, a great success at the Bar. He had very large practice. He did his work meticulously and was most unassuming. He too was raised to the Bench and ended his career by adorning the position of the Chief Justice of the Supreme Court. I had an occasion to engage him in a criminal appeal and we both had gone to Matheran, a hill-station near Bombay where I did briefing to him. We walked down the whole distance from Matheran to Neral, where we boarded the train for Bombay. He was a nice gentleman, very polite and considerate.

There were other senior Advocates — Jathar and Madbhavi from Karnataka. Madbhavi was soft-spoken and very friendly to all of us. He was very popular and was quite a success at the Bar. He knew astrology and we juniors used to gather around him to know our future prospects.

Jathar spoke excellent English and generally argued with great effect. He was easy-going and because of his exacting nature, he did not succeed to the extent he should have, looking to his merits, and ended by becoming a member of Revenue Tribunal. There were other promising Advocates, my contemporaries like V. S. Desai, M. G. Chitale and D. V. Patel, all of whom were raised to the Bench in course of time. Perhaps, I also could have become a Judge of the High Court in due course, but my destiny led me elsewhere as mentioned earlier. Belvi, an advocate, full of wit and humour, easy-going was a close friend of mine. He had a good gift of the gab, made interesting public speeches, and eventually ended his career by being appointed as Presidency Magistrate in Bombay.

Daftary was known for his ready wit. Once he was arguing in a case of detention. A Govt. circular in the case referred to the rival communities. When asked by N.H.C. Coyajee, a Parsi Judge as to which were these rival communities, Daftary replied that Parsis were the most unrivalled community and the reference in the circular meant only Hindus and Muslims. In another case before Judge Somjee Daftari cited some case and handed over the volume to the judge. There was one bug noticed in the volume; when the Judge made reference to it, Daftari observed that nowadays the bugs also have become ambitious and they want to scramble on to the Bench. It was dig at Somjee who was making uncharitable remarks against Daftari. Sir Chimanlal Setalwad, arguing an application for revision, when asked about the law point involved, said that there was no law point in the case, but his client wanted his Lordship's opinion. Jinnah, arguing an application for a certificate under 'Letters Patent' was asked about the substantial question of law involved, but he countered by observing whether the judge implied that there was no question of law when the judgement ran into 200 pages. So saying he sat down laughing. I think that Sir Chimanlal once enquired with his advocate whether the Bench was of 10 — meaning thereby that the other judge was a cipher.

I had a very good time in the High Court and enjoyed my legal career, short though it was, fully. We used to gather in the corridor, between cases and once Bhulabhai gave a hint that India was going to be partitioned on the basis of principle of self-determination. So it was.

While in the High Court we had an interesting programme at Malad in the bungalow of a senior Advocate, Ram Datta Desai. We, members of the appellate side Bar, juniors and seniors alike, gathered at his bungalow in the morning and spent the whole day and the night there. It was an excellent example of the spirit of camaraderie between seniors and juniors forgetting their high position and status in the society. We played cricket in the morning, had an excellent lunch in the afternoon, followed by rest and recreation. At night, we had arranged a programme of a kind of "लावणी, मुजरा संगीत" accompanied by expressive gestures based mostly on Lord Krishna's childhood plays and pranks. The star performer was the well-known Menaka of Belgaum, dancer and singer, who was exceedingly beautiful and accomplished. The programme was so good and captivating that the audience which included highly respected seniors remained glued to their seats till early morning in spite of their commitments of public engagements the following morning. We, juniors, of course enjoyed thoroughly.

Dajisaheb Tuljapurkar had a very spacious bungalow at Malawali, a wayside station, on the Bombay-Poona railway line. We, advocates of the appellate side numbering about 50 or so, had gone there on a trip on invitation from Dajisaheb. Seniors like M. M. Kane, R. A. Jahagirdar had also joined. We spent the morning trekking the hill-side, followed by lunch and rest in the afternoon. In the evening, we had a sort of campfire outside, in the courtyard of the bungalow. Dajisaheb was an excellent host and he provided everything for our comfort and convenience. We returned to Bombay the next day. Dajisaheb had a distinguished personality and was quite social and mixed freely with the young and old alike. V. D. Tuljapurkar, a judge of the Supreme Court (retd) is his son. He was the author of well-known book in Marathi, *Majhe Ramayan.*

Before leaving the High Court. I must mention about the gorgeous ceremony in the High Court, on the night of August 14, 1947, when India became free. Sir Leonard Stone, with all his regalia accompanied by Lady Stone, a handsome personality in Indian saree, made a short and solemn speech to end exactly at the stroke of mid-night. All the judges and the Advocate-general in their official robes and officers of the High Court including me dressed likewise, had gathered together in the Central Court (where sessions used to be held) where this function took place. It was a memorable occasion and the whole thing was planned in a manner worthy of the great occasion. My elder sister Kamlakka had come to Bombay and watched me from the gallery, where she was seated, with a sense of pride and importance of the occasion.

Chapter V

LEGISLATIVE SERVICE AND WORK

How I came to be drafted to the Legislature makes an interesting story. I was getting impatient and restless because of my having to remain as Dy. Registrar too long. I was looking out for an opening and breakthrough. I did not see any. To go back to the Bar seemed to be the only course open to me. I had spoken to my friends and others about this position. R. S. Hukkerikar, who was then the Chairman of the Bombay Legislative Council came to my rescue. The post of the Secretary to the Legislature had to be filled in. Sheode who was the Secretary then, was already under extension and the authorities desired the post to be filled in by a new person having both judicial and administrative experience. The post required a person with a sound knowledge of the Constitution and Law, combined with administrative experience and above all, with a background of independence, to be able to hold the scales even between Govt. and the opposition.

The Legislature was supreme in its allotted field under the Constitution and the Govt. was responsible and accountable to it, for what it did or did not do. Bombay State as it then was, had a bicameral legislature (Legislative Assembly and Legislative

Council) under 1935 Govt. of India Act, whose powers were limited and the Govt. still reigned supreme. The post of the Secretary to the Legislature was generally filled by an officer of the legal department of Govt. usually an I.C.S. officer. K. C. Sen, N. K. Dravid, H. K. Chainani and V. N. Sardesai, all I.C.S., were the secretaries among others, during pre-independence days. But with the passing of the Indian Independence Act 1947, India became free, and Indian Legislatures came to acquire the position and status consistent with the new Constitutional requirements. Sheode, my predecessor, an officer of the Law Department was the Secretary of the then Bombay Legislature, which still functioned as of old and there was an urgent need to change all this and bring its working in tune with the new constitutional position. Sheode tried to do this as much as possible but the progress of change was long and arduous, especially because the executive was reluctant to adjust itself to the new situation. The Authorities therefore — especially, the Speaker of the Legislative Assembly and the Chairman of the Legislative Council were in search of a suitable person for the job. Morarjee Desai, who was then the Chief Minister of Bombay, agreed with this but left the matter largely to be handled by the Speaker and the Chairman. They had already made a short list of the eligible persons for the post.

Mr. Justice Chagla, the new Chief Justice had arranged a small reception for his daughter's marriage on the lawns of his official bungalow on Malabar Hill and I was invited to this reception, being one of the senior officers of the Court. D. K. Kunte, the Speaker was also there. He consulted Mr. Justice Tendolkar, a judge of fierce independence, and possibly also a Congress sympathizer. He was wearing, even in those days, clothes made of Khadi. Kunte naturally was drawn towards him and took him in confidence and showed him the short list which they had made.

When they came to my name which must have been included at Hukkerikar's (Chairman, Legislative Council) suggestion, Mr. Justice Tendolkar told Kunte emphatically that there was no need to look further as Belavadi was the best person who filled the bill completely. He even volunteered to procure the Chief Justice's permission to release him for the job with a good chit. Kunte had therefore no other option in the matter. Mr. Justice Tendolkar sent word to me through his Chopdar, as I had no phone connection then and I went and saw him the next day morning. He told me all that had happened and said that only the paper work remained for the appointment to materialize.

I thanked him for this unexpected stroke of good-luck. The whole thing happened behind the back of Mr. Justice Gajendragadkar, who, though an administrative judge, had no role to play in this. Before I took charge of the new appointment, I called on Gajendragadkar in his chamber to bid him good-bye. He asked me why I was leaving the High Court, to which I replied that I was going to a better post than the registrar's post, which had been denied to me for too long. Gajendragadkar always professed friendship and concern for me but I do not know why he acted otherwise. However, in order to give an opening to me, the High Court recommended me for appointment as an Assistant Judge, but it did not materialize as Morarjee, the Chief Minister did not approve of it since the proposal was a departure from the normal practice, which required the recruitment to the post of Assistant Judge, either by promotion from the Sub-Judges or directly through the Bar. Somehow the proposals from the High Court in the administrative matters were not given due weight as it was perhaps thought that they were the handiwork of Gajendragadkar, who did not seem to command much clout in the Govt. Any way, my career in the High Court came to an end — and my new life began in the Legislative field.

My initial years with Kunte as Speaker were not happy. But for the support Hukkerikar, the Chairman of Legislative Council and Morarjee Desai, as the Chief Minister, extended to me I could not have continued there. Kunte was a difficult man to work with. Perhaps he expected me to be at his service, all the time as his personal secretary. I was brought up in the free and liberal atmosphere of the High Court, first as an Advocate and then as Dy. Registrar. I was quite prepared to do my best and be accountable for the work that legitimately fell within the scope of the job I held as the Secretary to the Legislature. I felt like the person who was given a long list of duties to be performed by him, added with the rider, "so far as it goes, so far as it goes it does not go far enough. There are many more duties which a person aspiring to be a Secretary to a Member of Parliament must never lose sight of," a humourous description given in the 'Spectator' by Charles Dickens about the job of a Secretary to a Member of Parliament.

I could not come up to his expectations. Kunte started harassing me, and even insulting me in all ways. He was rude to the extreme. He would expect me to be standing before him all the time whenever he called me to his chamber for any work and would not allow me to take a seat. I was new to the post and was getting acquainted with the duties I was required to perform, while Kunte had been there for a much longer time before me, and it was easier for him to find fault in my work.

In the circumstances, I told Morarjee Desai that I would like to go back to the High Court as it was becoming increasingly difficult to continue there. Morarjee advised me to do no such thing and continue in the job faithfully while assuring that he would see that no harm was done to me. Morarjee was as good as his word and protected me in every way. He had even told me that Kunte was not going to be continued after his term was over. Kunte was very unpopular in the Govt. and he had no friends in the Ministry except Hiray. He had a knack of making enemies. He had become a Parliamentary Secretary along with Gulzarilal Nanda, and Y. B. Chavan, who rose to high positions while he stagnated. For this, he was himself entirely to blame. Because of this reputation even a wrong committed by me was easily condoned. He would have been relieved earlier but it was not the Congress policy to remove a person elected by them. They would rather allow the person to retire by efflux of time after his term was over without creating any controversy about the matter.

At one time Kunte even threatened to resign on this issue: but Morarjee told him to go ahead and he would accept his resignation rather than ask me to go back. Of course Kunte never gave his letter of resignation. Then Kunte tried to stop or delay my confirmation but there also he failed. I was confirmed in my due time in spite of his serious objection, and the copy of the confirmation order was sent to him for his information.

As a matter of fact, it was not necessary to send my case to the Public Service Commission for concurrence, but it was done so deliberately so as to make the decision beyond all challenge. Bhansali, the Chief Secretary, wrote the confirmation note in my own bungalow before sending it to P.S.C. for concurrence. Kunte had drawn up a sort of charge-sheet against me to dub me as incompetent and unfit to hold the post. I procured a copy of his so-called indictment and noted my reply to it point by point, which was accepted and went as the opinion of Hukkerikar, the Chairman of Legislative Council, as against Kunte's. P.S.C. concurred with Hukkerikar's opinion and Morarjee Desai had no difficulty to uphold my confirmation. His indictment against me was hollow and baseless.

Once Kunte ceased to be the Speaker after the Madras Conference of Speakers in 1956, I had no reason to look back and went ahead from strength to strength in the remaining long period of nearly two decades of service. I was able to do some solid work by way of reforms in Legislative procedures and build up an efficient secretariat to serve the two houses without fear or favour in a manner contemplated under the Constitution.

I came to the legislature in 1953 and continued there till 1978 for over a quarter of a century. From 1953 to 1972 I was the Secretary to the Legislature and then for a period of five years as a Secretary of Dept. of Legislative Affairs. I organized the Dept. of Legislative Affairs on the lines of the Ministry of Parliamentary Affairs at the Centre to advise Govt. in legislative matters on one hand and act as a Liaison between the Govt. and the Legislature on the other. It was during this long period that I did my life's most precious work, which looking back at this distance of time, was highly satisfying and rewarding. This constituted my best and lasting contribution in the legislative field to which a detailed reference will be made in the pages to follow.

In order to understand the nature, importance and amplitude of my work, as Secretary to the Legislature, it would be necessary to make a brief reference to the Constitutional position, bearing on Govt. and the legislature. Indian Constitution provides for a Federation, consisting of the states and the Union each having a parliamentary form of Govt. based on the British model. There would be elections every five years based on adult franchise. The majority would form the Govt. and the others would work as the opposition.

The Govt. whether in the Union or the States must have a majority to support it all the time and would be responsible and accountable to the concerned Legislature for all its commissions and omissions. The Constitution has demarcated powers and functions between the States and the Union and each House of the Legislature is provided with a secretariat to enable it to exercise its powers and functions under the Constitution. The secretariat is controlled and administered by a joint Board of Chairman, Legislative Council, and Speaker, Legislative Assembly, in the States and by the Speaker and the Chairman of each House of Parliament separately at the centre. The Secretariat is headed by a Secretary, who is assisted by a staff consisting of officers and other personnel to enable him to discharge his functions.

What are the functions of the Secretary? They are three-fold:

1. To attend to the work of the Legislature,

2. To advise the Speaker, Legislative Assembly and the Chairman, Legislative Council on matters coming before the House, and

3. To look after the administration of the secretariat as its head, under the overall control of the Speaker and the Chairman.

The Legislature itself has triple functions:

a. Legislation i.e. to make Laws,

b. Financial i.e. to pass the budget etc.

c. To exercise the function of criticism, on the omissions and commissions of govt., which is continuous during the Sessions.

There are elaborate rules formed by the House itself to regulate these matters by proper procedures so as to enable the Legislature to discharge effectively its functions under the Constitution.

In pre-independence days the Legislature enjoyed limited powers and Govt. was supreme. The position changed with independence with the result that the Legislature in its allotted field, was supreme and the Govt. was responsible to it. The procedural rules had to be changed in a big way to reflect this change and to enable the Legislature to discharge its Constitutional powers and functions. The Legislature — secretariat, which assists the Legislature in the discharge of these functions had to be independent and not subordinate to Govt., as was the position previously. In other words the whole thing had to be changed to bring it in line with the Constitution. We were assisted in this, in a big way, by the conference of Presiding Officers which, under the dynamic personality of late G. V. Mavlankar, the Speaker of Lok Sabha and its president, guided through its annual conferences, all the legislative bodies in the country, in the matter of procedural rules and independence of the Legislature secretariat. This conference was our inspiration and guide and we set about doing work, towards that end. (See Appendix V).

We directed our attention first to 'Public Accounts Committee' and 'Committee on Estimates' the only two committees functioning then, which were formed and working contrary to all principles of parliamentary practice and procedure. The P.A.C. was headed by the minister for finance which was wrong. Its secretarial functions were performed by the Secretary, finance, which was again wrong. The work of this committee consists in the examination of accounts and expenditure of Govt. to see whether there are any financial or budgetary irregularities, whether money voted for a particular service has been utilized for that service and not diverted elsewhere, whether the spending has been wise and economical; and excess expenditure, i.e. spending more than the sanctioned amount which is also gone into, so as to regularize it in due course, by Vote of the Legislature. The basis of the examination are the reports of the Comptroller and Auditor General of India which go into all kinds of financial and budgetary irregularities, besides looking into the wisdom of spending in any particular matter.

In all these things Govt. is the spending authority and it is obviously wrong to have the Finance Minister and the Finance Secretary in a position to control its working. The correct practice is to have a Finance Minister of the out going ministry as the Chairman of the Committee, the secretarial functions being performed by the secretary of the Legislature, who is independent of Govt. Jivraj Mehta who was the

Minister for Finance, then, was not willing to give up the Chairmanship of the committee for obvious reasons. Not only that he would not even allow the reports of the Comptroller and Auditor General of India to be placed before the Legislature as required by the Constitution, unless and until they were examined by P.A.C. of which he was the Chairman. Thus he would ensure that all larger matters of serious nature were glossed over and only minor matters were highlighted for public consumption.

First, we had to wage a battle for getting the reports placed before the Legislature as soon as they were ready. In this, we were helped by the Comptroller and Auditor General of India himself who was equally keen as we were. Ultimately Silam, the Speaker of Legislative Assembly, had to threaten the Finance Minister that he would get the reports placed before the House through the Legislature Secretary, if he failed or objected to their placing. Jivraj Mehta had to yield and the reports were duly placed before the House. Secretarial functions had already been taken over by the Secretary, Legislature, under orders of the Speaker Kunte earlier. But the functioning of the committee continued as before as Jivraj Mehta, the Minister of Finance, still continued to be the Chairman. This had to be changed and was changed eventually when Wankhede became the Minister for Finance and he, of his own, gave up the Chairmanship of the committee and a non-official member from the opposition came to be appointed as Chairman of the Committee.

An interesting case occurred in respect of a contract known as jawai contract concerning the construction of tube-wells in North Gujarat. There were serious financial irregularities apart from the capacity of the company — technical and financial, to construct the wells and Govt. could be legitimately blamed for the resulting loss. Jivraj Mehta, as the Chairman, did a hat-trick by producing a report which comprised extracts favourable to Govt. from the reports prepared by Accountant-General, Secretary, Legislature and Secretary, Finance. Even so the Govt. had to accept the blame for what it did. G. S. Rao, who was then the Accountant-General of the state was fair, reasonable, and soft spoken but quite firm in his views and opinions. He did not like the way the report was made but he did not stretch his opposition too far.

Similar was the case with the Committee on Estimates. It used to examine only the staff position and make minor recommendations in that respect. The real object of the Committee is to examine the budget estimates and suggest economy and efficiency in their spending to get the best results. Here also, we had to wait until the committee was headed by a non-official member instead of the Minister for Finance. Again Wankhede came to our rescue. We then turned our attention to see what other committees were needed to ensure parliamentary control.

We decided to set up immediately the following three committees to ensure proper control of the administration.

i Subordinate Legislation Committee.

ii Committee on Govt Assurances.

iii Committee on Public Undertakings.

The Committee on Subordinate Legislation or delegated Legislation, examines to see if the Govt. or any other executive authority, while making rules, under the Rule-Making Section of the Parent Act, has exceeded its authority. The rules to be made are of an ancillary or procedural nature to administer the Act properly and effectively. But it was noticed that Govt. often travelled beyond its powers and the rules thus made being a part of the Law could not be challenged except by Court action. The Committee sees that the authority vested in the Govt. by legislation is not in any way exceeded. Besides, the rule-making sections in the various acts of the Legislature were not uniform and often gave powers far beyond the purposes and sometimes even overriding the Act itself. The Committee was therefore quite necessary to check and correct these excesses. The Committee was set up and it did very commendable work.

To start with, it made two very important recommendations; (I) It introduced model clauses for rule-making powers which ensured uniformity and legislative control. The Govt. accepted this and agreed to amend all the Acts, in due course, which was done. (II) The other recommendation clearly demarcated the fields of legislation and subordinate legislation. This was necessary because very often the rules made by Govt. were of the nature of substantive legislation. This greatly helped the Committee in its work. We were also able to set up the other two Committees, viz. Committee on Govt. Assurances and Committee on Public Undertakings. The purpose of the Committee on Govt. Assurances is to see that the assurances given by the Govt. in the House are duly and promptly fulfilled. The Committee on Public Undertakings like State Transport, Electricity Board, etc. examines and makes recommendations for their efficient and economic working, without interfering in their day-to-day work. Then in due course, several other

Committees were set up of varying importance to ensure proper control by the Legislature, of the Executive. The necessary rules were made in rules of procedure including rules for their internal working.

We then turned our attention to the question procedure. The questions put to the Govt. were not answered promptly. Govt. took its own time to answer questions. We introduced a system, as in the House of Commons in U.K. or in Parliament, in Delhi, so that questions were answered on stated days and members knew when their questions would come up for answers. When the system was first introduced in the Nagpur Session, I was flooded with requests from Ministers and Secretaries to the Govt. to postpone their questions on the allotted days as it was not possible to answer them on those days. My stock answer was that Minister should tell the House to that effect. This worked as nobody wanted to face the House and say that he was not ready to answer the question. The system started working smoothly thereafter. This was an important step in the way of reforms, and it was accomplished by our persuasive and persistent efforts. We then introduced a number of what are called parliamentary devices to enable the Legislature to exercise its power of criticism on Govt.'s commissions and omissions. We made elaborate rules for their governance.

But all this process was spread over a period of time encountering opposition from the executive, which was firmly entrenched in its position. I got full cooperation and support from my Speaker, S. L. Silam and Chairman V. S. Page, Yashwantrao Chavan and after him Kannamwar and Vasantrao Naik, the successive Chief Ministers, despite opposition from other ministers like Law Minister Shantilal Shah and of course, the Secretaries to Govt. When the Committee on Subordinate Legislation was set up, much against the wishes of Law Minister Shantilal Shah, he as the Chairman of the Committee, made it well-nigh impossible for its proper working by asking us to follow a difficult procedure, which would lead us nowhere. But there also we devised a method to which he had to agree, and our work proceeded smoothly. In course of time, we saw to it with the active help of the Speaker and Chief Minister, that he ceased to be the Chairman, but remained only a member of the Committee. When Antulay became the Chairman, he made his presence almost nugatory. Shantilal used to bring the Law Secretary to advise him but Antulay stopped it by saying that Shantilal was only a member of the Committee and not a Law Minister there. He even ordered the removal of the Board 'Law Minister' before him. Shantilal then himself resigned from the Committee. Credit must go to the dynamic and courageous Antulay to make the working of the Committee a big success.

In the Committees — P.A.C. and E. C. of which the Minister for Finance Jivraj Mehta was the Chairman, the work was not done as expected from a Parliamentary Committee. He would sit long hours, tire out the members and get the results as he wanted. This was so especially in P.A.C. Jivraj Mehta was an indefatigable worker, spared no pains for himself and for others who worked with him. Members would get tired soon and leave everything to him. He would even enquire from me while tea and snacks were being served to the members, which of the members took milk and not tea. He was strict and authoritarian. I had good rapport and relations with him, though I did not like his methods and attitude to the Legislature.

In the Rules Committee, we had to contend with the opposition of Law Minister Shantilal Shah. He would object and obstruct the much needed reforms in the procedural rules. We had to make a water-proof case for every proposed change so that he could not object. We overhauled rules of procedure in a big way so as to bring it in tune with the correct parliamentary position.

One of the old rules permitted Govt. to publish a bill in a Gazette, as L. A. Bill or L. C. Bill without L. A. or L. C. knowing anything about it. The new rule provided that a bill cannot be so published in a Gazette unless it was introduced first in L. A. or L. C. As an expedient, Govt. was permitted to publish the bill after getting the required permission from the Speaker or the Chairman. Shantilal Shah, the Law Minister, was a party to the change. Even so, when the rule came into force, it created a furore among the Govt. departments and Shantilal feigned ignorance. A meeting was called at the residence of the C. M. without telling us what the meeting was about. However we gathered the required information and were ready for the conference. But they i.e. Law Minister, Chief Secretary, Law Secretary did not discuss the point but started a tirade against me personally to poison the mind of the C.M. I was not allowed to defend myself nor Bharade, my Speaker would say anything. However C. M. had nothing against me, of which Bharade seemed sure. Perhaps C. M. agreed to call the meeting to let the steam off.

Another case — a very interesting case, worthy of notice occurred in connection with the custody of bills passed by the Legislature. We claimed the custody instead of the Law Department of Govt. as the rightful custodian. Formerly, Law Department kept the custody because Legislature Secretariat had not come into being. But this was objected, too. In the conference with C.M., Law Minister and others, it was agreed that one set of authenticated bills should be given to us for custody, provided the President of India agreed to sign additional copies where his assent was necessary. The dept. of Govt., i.e. Law Dept., knew from our file in the case that the President had refused to sign additional copies, when the question was raised earlier before him. Speaker Silam, in good faith, had left our file with them for the necessary orders. That is how that they had come to know about the President's refusal in the matter. Since the President's consent was not available, Govt. refused to agree to our proposal even with regard to bills to be signed by the Governor. We waited for a proper opportunity to meet the President and obtain his consent. Soon the opportunity came, when the President visited Poona. Silam and Page, the Speaker, and the Chairman went to Poona and met the President in the presence of the governor Sri Prakasa with our case ready with proper noting, supported by authorities and practices in other parliaments.

The President readily agreed to our request and orders were issued which were applicable all over India. For such a small thing though fully right and proper, we had to struggle so much. Sri Prakasa, the Governor, helped us a great deal in this respect.

There was a question of putting up portraits of the leaders of the Nation in the Assembly Hall in Bombay. We had already taken a decision that no portraits should be put up in the Assembly Hall, following the example of the House of Commons in England. We had made an exception only in the case of Mahatma

Gandhi. Normally only the head of the State alone is given that honour, like the Queen in England or the President of India here. After a lot of discussion, amidst various claims put up by different parties, we decided that the portraits of a few selected leaders—builders of the Nation should be put up in the Lobby of the Council Hall. We also decided to transfer these portraits to the Central Hall of the New Council Hall building, when it was ready, as in New Delhi.

Maneckji, the aviation advisor to Govt., had created some difficulty for us. He had his own private air-company and he was suspected of having used his official position for his personal benefit. He would write to the Govt. of India that the State Govt. did not need a hangar for Govt. aircraft and would himself take it later for his aircraft. It was suspected that there was some misuse of Govt. petrol. The Accountant-General Nair, wished to bring this out. Maneckji, aviation advisor to Govt. would not even show the concerned files, to which the Accountant-General was entitled under the law. We both decided to take up this matter before P.A.C. and prepared the report after due examination in the Committee. But someone, obviously an interested person, carried *tales* to the C. M. that I had changed some portion in the report, to bring out the guilt clearly. C. M. questioned me about this and I told him that it was not true and I was prepared to show him all the drafts for his satisfaction. But the C. M. did not desire to pursue the matter further and the matter was allowed to rest there. Our report however was implemented by Govt. though they did not say so in the implementation report. We had strongly recommended against the practice of appointing a person functioning in a dual capacity, where there was a possibility of conflict between his private and public interests. This was accepted.

In another case concerning the Civil supplies Department there were some serious irregularities in the procurement and distribution of foodgrains. P.A.C. decided to go deeper into the matter and appointed a sub-committee for its examination. We wanted the relevant files from the Govt. for examination. Files however were not forthcoming. I contacted the Secretary of the Dept. and asked him whether he wanted the order of the Chairman of the Committee or of the Speaker for it. He said that it would not make any difference. However, on the day of examination, Govt. realized the position and agreed to send the files. But it was too late. We took the files — but did no examination on that day and adjourned the meeting with the remark that because of the recalcitrant attitude taken by the Dept. in the matter, the meeting had become infructuous. On the next date of hearing, Bhirud, the Chairman of the Committee, castigated the Secretary, for their unreasonable and untenable stand in the matter. The work then proceeded and our report did have a good effect on the administration and the Govt. took necessary steps to remedy the matter.

Late Dr. R. G. Ginde was neurosurgeon of great international renown. He had a massive heart-attack, while still in the prime of his youth with the result that he had to suspend his vast practice in Bombay and outside. When he recovered, he was advised to curtail his practice because of his recent illness. Shantilal Shah who was then the Minister for Health asked Dr. Ginde to organise a Dept. of Neurology, under the State Govt., which would extend to him every help that was needed. He would be paid an honorarium of Rs. 2000/- p.m. as the Director of the Dept. Dr. Ginde agreed to this and accepted the offer. But this was not liked by other honoraries serving under the Govt. They started a sort of non-cooperation with Govt. and tried to pressurise Govt. to undo the thing. Ginde was greatly handicapped for want of necessary staff and other facilities like telephone, accommodation, etc., to organise and run the Directorate.

In the meantime Zakaria had become the Minister of Health. Ginde was our family friend and he mentioned his difficulty to me. I tried to help him through the good offices of Zakaria but it did not work. Zakaria was just helpless, though he sympathized with the cause, because of the body of honoraries who were adamant in their attitude. The Estimates Committee came to our rescue. While examining the Health Dept. of Govt. they noticed this apathy and neglect of Govt. and came down heavily on Govt. for their deplorable inaction and yielding to the pressure tactics of the honoraries. The press also took notice of this injustice and wrote strong editorials against Govt. Ginde greatly appreciated this and felt that his reputation, which was at stake, was fully restored. This is a glaring example to show how Govt. are pressurised and held to ransom for satisfying minor interests. This also shows how the press can help a genuine cause in a big way. But the main help came from E.C. which upheld the cause, without fear or favour of anybody. Zakaria blamed me initially for this onslaught on the Govt. but later relented on realizing the true position. The E.C. did commendable work during my time and made far reaching recommendations to improve the administration.

Here I must also mention the commendable work done by the Committee on Privileges to uphold the dignity and the authority of the Legislature. The following three cases stand out in my memory even today for the great public interest they generated and also because they covered different aspects of privileges.

Bhabha Hospital building had collapsed while still under construction. For this, the Bombay Municipal Administration came under heavy attack in the Assembly in a debate on the subject. The whole Municipal administration was characterized as corrupt from top to bottom. The press gave it a lot of publicity the next day. The Bombay Municipal Corporation then held a special meeting and strongly criticized the speakers in the Assembly debates. This also received a lot of publicity in the press.

A privilege motion was promptly moved by P. G. Kher in the Assembly for violation of the privilege of freedom of speech against the Corporators including the Mayor Madhavan and the Corporation itself. All of them were held guilty for this gross breach of privilege of the Members and the House after due examination in the Committee. The case was fought at great length in the Committee, with the help of eminent advocates — Advocate-General and others. The Corporation was fined Rs.10,000/- and the Corporators including the Mayor were called upon to tender an unqualified apology, or otherwise face the resultant punishment. A lot of political pressure was brought on the C. M. Vasantrao Naik to drop the proceedings since they were also elected members of a large City Corporation whose budget ran into several hundred crores.

I impressed upon the C. M. not to yield in the matter as it would set up a bad precedent and the Legislature stood to lose its prestige and authority in public estimation. It must be realized that the Legislature and the Corporation cannot be treated on the same footing, as the former enjoys special privileges under the Constitution whereas the later has no such privileges, however big it may be. The C. M. accepted this view and the corporators had to tender an unqualified apology before they were let off. The fine against the Corporation also was remitted.

In another case involving contempt of the House, the *Times of India* and its then editor Frank Moraes stood charged with the offence for an editorial entitled 'contemptible' in one of its issues. A notice of breach of privilege and contempt of the House was promptly tabled by one Ambalal Shah against the paper for the editorial in question, which had severely criticized the conduct of the House and its unworthy members, for tabling a question on 'liquor permits', and for further eliciting the names of the judges of the Bombay High Court, having the Liquor permits, through a supplementary. Those were prohibition days and under Morarjee's rule, it was enforced strictly. After due examination, in the Committee of Privileges the paper and its editor Frank Moraes were held guilty and it was decided to admonish the editor and also withdraw the press facilities of the paper, until it tendered an unqualified apology for the offence. The admonition was administered by Speaker Silam to Frank Moraes who stood at the Bar of the House to receive it. The case made big head lines in the press and the whole proceeding was conducted with great dignity and solemnity. It was one of the earliest cases on 'privilege' and the entire conduct of the case was organised with meticulous care and attention. S. M. Joshi was then newly elected to the Assembly and he was one of the members of the Committee. He voted with Govt. which was greatly appreciated by Morarjee Desai, the then C.M. In privilege matters it is wrong to divide on party-lines — as the privileges concern the House as a whole. S. M. Joshi therefore had acted correctly. The paper *'Times of India'* did not tender an apology for a long time. But it continued to enjoy the press facilities through its other paper *'Evening News'*. When the House was dissolved after its term and a new House was constituted, the paper thought that it would now claim press facilities in its own right, as the old Assembly had been dissolved along with its offence against it. But we stood firm and maintained that the offence could not be wiped out until an apology was given, after taking the opinion of the Advocate-General. The paper then apologized and press facilities were restored. This was a case where an affront was made to the Legislature, by a direct attack on its dignity and authority giving rise to the offence of contempt.

In yet another case, notice of breach of privilege and contempt was tabled by Mandani against P. K. Atre, for his article in his paper *'Maratha'* entitled '420 Mamdani'. The article had criticized Mamdani for his alleged conduct in defrauding Govt. in some matter. The offence concerned private conduct of the member and it in no way interfered with his Parliamentary duties. But we admitted it and sent it to the Committee for examination. In this Committee a whole review of the Case-Law on the subject was made and it confirmed our view on the question. It is one of the important reports where a whole Case-Law on the subject is discussed confirming the position that private conduct of a member cannot be the subject matter of any privilege. Atre when informed of the decision of the Committee was greatly pleased and said so in so many words.

Bhirud, a renowned lawyer from Jalgaon, did his work as the Chairman of P.C. with considerable tact and ability and he was always a great asset to us. His name will always be remembered as the chairman of the Committee on privileges in several important cases including the one I have referred to above. He was basically a committee-man and his contribution in the Committee work was solid, whether in a Committee of privileges or Public Accounts. He was very friendly with me and we carried on the work in a spirit of camaraderie with great effect.

Of the Legislative proceedings, the following stand upper-most in my mind, namely, the great debate, if acrimonious, on the reorganization Bill, sent to the legislative Assembly for its opinion, discussion of 'labour' demands as priority No.1 in the discussion of demands for grants, debate on the adjournment motion following the visit of Pandit Nehru to Pratapgad, the condolence resolution on the demise of Pandit Nehru, the Prime Minister and the discussion on Hiray's Bill (land to the tiller). In the debate on the Reorganization Bill speeches made by Y. B. Chavan, B. S. Hiray, Ghate and of course the C. M. Morarjee Desai may be mentioned. In spite of strong feelings on the question of inclusion of Bombay city in Maharashtra, the Congress Party behaved by and large in a disciplined manner. Hiray complained that the Koyna Project was going to benefit only the capitalists by taking away the lands of poor persons, to produce electricity. Morarjee's reply was mainly confined to meet the charges made by Hiray. Morarjee began by asserting that Hiray was speaking today because he (Morarjee) had permitted him to do so. Hiray was then considered to be the only rebel in Morarjee's Cabinet, for urging formation of Maharashtra with Bombay city included in it. Morarjee explained that there could not be irrigation of lands in Maharashtra with Koyna water as perhaps thought by Hiray, which is an engineering fact. The lands in Bijapur District in Karnataka would be irrigated with that water. He declared that Hiray or any other minister or ministers were free to plead or urge before the High Command for acceptance of their view. But he would not agree to place their views as his views before them. Later on, when I went to Chiplun from Karad I could see the truth of Morarjee's statement. The mile stones on the old caravan route, mentioned the distance to Bijapur. Y. B. Chavan's speech was a model of literary piece, persuasive and convincing. He was not much in the picture then. On the whole the debate was carried on with dignity and decorum, in spite of high feelings on the subject.

Shantilal Shah was the Labour Minister and the opposition desired to discuss 'Labour' for two days, as their first priority, while discussing demands for grants. Members of the Opposition, Socialist and Communists, discussed the question at great length and tried to find fault with the Govt. in all manner of ways. Shantilal Shah spoke at the end for just half an hour and tore their arguments to smithereens and almost held them to ridicule by saying that they did now know what a Trade Union was or its functions and they only indulged in fomenting and fighting litigation, quoting chapter and verse. The opposition was completely silenced. Shantilal held the view and rightly so, that disputes must be taken to the

Conciliation Board first and if they did not get justice there, they could approach the Govt. But if they resorted to strikes without going through this procedure, the Govt. would not go to their rescue.

He was quite firm in that view. He was an accomplished parliamentarian, and would end his speech exactly within his allotted time. He was precise and somewhat legalistic in his attitude. On the whole, he was very effective. He was respectful to the Chair and observed all the rules of conduct meticulously. He was a keen lawyer and well-versed in the rules of procedure. He would be remembered for the laws on 'Public Undertakings Relief' and 'Labour Welfare Fund'. Once while answering a question, he replied in such a way that the opposition could get nothing out of it, while all the time remaining within the rules.

Pandit Jawaharlal Nehru was paying a visit to Pratapgad to garland the statue of Chhatrapati Shivaji Maharaj installed there. The atmosphere was surcharged with high feelings because of the burning question of Samyukta Maharashtra with the city of Bombay included in it. We had a morning session of the Legislature on that day and the atmosphere there reflected the position obtaining outside. S. M. Joshi was leading the opposition outside for impressing on Nehru the strong feelings of the State in the matter. He made a fiery speech on the Motion of adjournment — tabled in the House. Y. B. Chavan was C.M. then and he handled the situation both inside and outside the House, with great tact, forbearance and patience. Joshi spoke with obvious sincerity which immediately touched the hearts of the people. He was a good speaker. More than his oratory, his sincerity of purpose and courage of conviction, made a great impact. He was one of the few leaders of the opposition, respected and admired by the Treasury Benches. The matter passed off smoothly without any untoward incident because of the patience, tact and understanding attitude of Y.B. Chavan.

In the Monsoon Session in Pune we passed a bill known as Hiray's Bill which passed the ownership of lands to the tenants. Dutta Deshmukh made a marathon speech, on its first reading lasting several days. It must be the longest speech in the history of Legislative Assembly. He was a good speaker, with a real compassion for the downtrodden. The session lasted for nearly 3 weeks and this bill took all the time, including the stage of the Select Committee and its further consideration thereafter. In those days, the House spent a great amount of time on Bills. They were not passed quickly — a trend developed later. It was a bill of far reaching importance, making the tiller the owner of the land. Similarly, we devoted one full session in Bombay for re-enacting the Sales-Tax Bill after the old one was declared null and void by the High Court in respect of some of the crucial clauses.

When Y. B. Chavan was invited to go to the Centre as the Minister for Defence following the war with China, there was a farewell function in the Assembly to bid him farewell. Two speeches made on that occasion, one by P. K. Atre and the other by Y. B. Chavan, the outgoing C. M. stand out. Atre praised Chavan for his ability, and capacity to handle difficult situations, and wished him luck and good wishes of the House, on his new assignment, which was by no means easy. It is a rare thing for a person to receive such fulsome praise and tribute, from an opposition leader in a legislative chamber. Chavan also spoke feelingly, forgetting the divide between the Treasury and the Opposition and the whole house acted with one voice in the matter. Chavan fondly observed that he was sorry to leave them and loved dearly each and everything in the House and things connected with it. It was a moving proceeding 'worthy of the occasion' Sahyadri going to the rescue of Himalaya.

I must also mention here questions asked in the House which were most difficult and complicated, on police firings in Bombay, following the agitation for 'संयुक्त महाराष्ट्र' by B. C. Kamble, a Republican Party Leader and on Panshet-dam-disaster, by Dutta Deshmukh. The former was characterized by the minute and complicated details of the various injuries caused by the firing while the latter was noted for the technical knowledge and skill, displayed by Dutta Deshmukh, himself, a civil engineer, in regard to the various technical details involved in the construction of the dam, its exit gates etc. It must be said in fairness to Morarjee Desai in the first and Jivraj Mehta in the second, who, as concerned Ministers, replied to these questions and the supplementaries thereto, with equal care and attention in a forthright manner. The proceedings of the days in question will reveal the depth and the skill with which questions were framed and replied with equal skill and ability.

V. N. Patil and Dutta Deshmukh, able and knowledgeable parliamentarians, though forming part of opposition, had their own identity, as belonging to a small party Lal Nishan. In any debate of importance after one of them spoke, the other would in his turn, supplement or add what was left out by the first. When procedural rules were being considered for reforms, these two stalwarts did their best to suggest changes that were needed, and rightly so. But Dinkarrao Desai, the Law Minister, did not even bother to explain the reasons, for their rejection. It seemed that he had set his face against any change. He was an able minister who knew the correctness of the proposed changes, but somehow, he did not want any changes then.

I cannot conclude this topic without making a reference to the Condolence Resolution, on the demise of Prime Minister Pandit Nehru, passed in the Assembly after two remarkable speeches made by P. K. Atre and Speaker T. S. Bharade. Atre made a brilliant speech. Barade as speaker spoke last, and it was no less brilliant. After the House adjourned after passing the resolution, we had gathered in the Speaker's Chamber when Atre told Bharade with obvious sincerity that Bharade's speech excelled his and congratulated him on that account. Atre had that greatness of mind and magnanimity, we were very much impressed by that. (Extracts of these are given in the Appendix II).

I was invited by the Secretary-General of C.P.A. Sir Howard De'Guill to the House of Commons for a Parliamentary Course conducted by them. I told Silam, Speaker, that I would go if the State Govt. paid for my journey, to and fro, the expenses in U.K. being borne by C.P.A. When Silam mentioned this to C.M. Chavan, he expressed his inability to support this proposal as there would be other cases of such nature, asking for this kind of help. Silam told me so and we decided to drop the matter. When in the Executive Committee meeting (C.P.A.) the matter came up for decision, we proposed K. K. Shah's name. C. M. immediately intervened and said that Belavadi should be sent and not any member. Members come and go and it was no use sending them. The Secretary would remain and his going would be beneficial and useful. When Jivraj Mehta, Finance Minister, asked for the cost, Deoji Ratansi, another powerful member, said that they would foot the bill if the Govt. had any difficulty. Mehta readily agreed to foot the bill. K. K. Shah later became Minister in the govt. of India and was also the Governor of Madras. This was a case of sheer good luck for me.

After Kunte's exit, my work in the Secretariat had become easy and smooth. I had the best of relations with the Speakers Silam, Bharade and the Chairman V. S. Page, and C. M. and other ministers — perhaps with the exception of Shantilal Shah, Law Minister, during the period of 2 decades. But I had not much difficulty in dealing with him also. When there was an invitation to go to New Zealand for C.P.A. Conference, Bharade asked me to go to the C.M. at once for his sanction. I could meet the C.M. at any time, without any difficulty. When I mentioned to him about the invitation, he wholeheartedly supported me. When he suggested that I should speak to Wankhede, Finance Minister, in the matter and I expressed my hesitation to do so, he immediately assured me not to worry and that I could proceed without any difficulty. He was exceedingly kind and helpful to me, whether in the matter of giving priority for purchase of a car or allotment of a flat. When I mentioned to him about my retirement in a short time, he flatly told me that I was not leaving so long as he was there i.e. at least 3/4 years more. He was C.M. for 10/11 years and we carried on smoothly without any hassles. The question of parity in pay with Govt. Secretaries was pending for a long time. Ultimately it was settled by Shankarrao Chavan, Minister for Legislative Affairs. Wankhede, Minister for Finance, agreed though perhaps reluctantly. But there was also the question about giving retrospective effect. Shankarrao was agreeable for the full period of 4 years when the pay was revised, while Wankhede said it should be from the date of the orders. C. M. Naik called me and asked me what he should do. It was so kind of him. I left it to him and retrospective effect was given for one year.

Before Vasantrao Naik, Kannamwar was C.M. He was a very astute politician. After Y. B. Chavan, Vasantrao Naik's name as next C. M. had been very much in the news. But Kannamwar, the Vidarbha leader, was not to be side-tracked. When some journalists from Vidarbha met me in the office, they said that they had no doubt about Kannamwar becoming the next C.M. and so it was. Kannamwar's tenure was short — but he was a man of the masses and was extremely popular. He was equally firm in his views and dealings. When there was a municipal sweepers strike in Bombay on the eve of the monsoon, he was very firm in dealing with the strikers. When Raj Narayan came from Delhi, apparently to help out the C.M., he was flatly told to go back and he could handle the situation without any difficulty. Raj Narayan who claimed to be Y. B. Chavan's emissary had to go back, unceremoniously. When the strike failed and was withdrawn due to the firm handling, C. M. Kannamwar declared that the strike had fizzled out — emphasizing the words — 'fizzled out'. He had robust common sense and he spoke Hindi in the House very effectively and convincingly. I had an excellent rapport with him. When we had a meeting at his residence in connection with some of our pending cases, he told the Chief

Secretary, N. T. Mone to pass orders as I desired since he knew that I would not make any wrong proposal. I, on my part, would take every care to make the proposal foolproof.

V. N. Lokur, our family friend had been selected as a Legal Advisor to the Govt of India. The State Govt. would not agree to release him from his post of Presidency Magistrate unless he resigned from the post. Lokur could not afford to do so, as he had already put in 8/9 years of service and he did not want to lose the benefit of such a long service. I told him to explore other avenues open to him before I could try to help him. When he came to me at last, saying that there was nothing he could do in the matter, I agreed to take him to Kannamwar, C. M. for his intervention. Kannamwar readily agreed to bail him out. It was so done. Lokur was able to join his new post for which he had been selected, while retaining the benefits of service, as Presidency Magistrate, he had already put in. The practice in this connection is based on the principle that a person could not be allowed to use his existing position as a stepping stone to better his prospects elsewhere. If he desired to go to another post, he must resign from the post and then go. He cannot have it both ways. But this was a discretionary matter and hence we could succeed, in spite of numerous precedents to the contrary.

During our Nagpur Session in Winter, there used to be a Music festival, where wellknown artists, singers and dancers performed. The State Govt. had started it and was held under the State's patronage. On one occasion — may be in 1962 or 1963, we — my wife and myself were as usual, witnessing the programme sitting in front. Bhimsen Joshi, now the celebrated Musician had already finished his singing on the previous day and I think, Vasantrao Deshpande, another wellknown Musician had commenced his singing. A little while later, Bhimsen arrived from behind and signalled to us to follow him, where he would, along with two others — Sangmeshwar Gurav and another singer from Karnataka — sing, in a private bungalow of one landlord Deshmukh. We went there in our car, following Bhimsen who was leading us on a scooter, musical equipment like 'Tabla, Peti', etc. being put in our car. After reaching the place, we sat down in the verandah of the bungalow and all the three started singing, together, a sort of joint performance. They sang for the whole night and gave us an exhibition of excellent classical music, with only two or three of us, as the audience. When dawn came, Bhimsen got up and went to the well, in the backyard, drew water from the well in a bucket and poured over himself once or twice and got ready to go to the airport for going to Calcutta, for another musical engagement there. This was a memorable occasion once in a lifetime where we were regaled with excellent fare of music very, very privately and exclusively.

I must mention with gratitude the case of my nephew (sister's son) Rajendra Dhumale, who was anxious to join the Medical course. His percentage of marks in I.Sc. (Inter Science) though quite good, was not good enough to secure admission in Bombay or Poona. My friend Zala, the then Director of the Haffkine Institute, told me that the state Govt. had 5 seats in the Medical College, in Kashmir and I could try for one of them. I approached Zakaria, our Health Minister in that connection and he kindly agreed to help. There was also the difficulty regarding his qualifying age. This was sorted out through the good offices of Antulay, Minister for Education. After passing the Ist M.B.B.S. exam. Rajendra had to be brought back to Bombay. This was again very kindly done by Zakaria. Rajendra passed the M.B.B.S. and M.D. exams of the Bombay University and also qualified for double F.R.C.S. (Ireland). He has now married an English girl and is happily settled in Kingslynn, England. He has since earned a good name and reputation and has been declared 'doctor of the year', a great honour. Had it not been for the timely help of Zakaria, and Antulay this would not have been possible.

Chapter VI
INTERNATIONAL CONFERENCES AND FOREIGN TOURS

I have attended international conferences of C.P.A. in Australia, and New Zealand and in Copy Right matters in Paris, France. Generally in C.P.A. conferences, the Secretaries of Parliament — Lok Sabha and Rajya Sabha — used to attend, the State Secretaries like me, would attend, one only, by rotation according to the seniority of the branch.

I attended the Conference in Canberra in Australia, by sheer luck. It was the turn of the Secretary of West Bengal Branch of C.P.A. being the senior-most among the Branches. Somehow or the other, the Secretary of Australia was informed by the Secretary, Lok Sabha Kaul, that Belavadi, the Maharashtra Secretary, should be invited, since he was not in a position to attend it. Silam, my Speaker, attended the Conference as a delegate representing Maharashtra Branch, and I attended it, as the Secretary of the entire delegation. Ananthasayanam Ayyangar was the leader of the delegation, being the Speaker of the Lok Sabha. Internal tours were an integral part of the Conference. So we toured the whole Australia, a country of kangaroos, twice as big in area as India. We were about 14 members from India and I was supposed, as the Secretary of the delegation, to arrange members for speeches on the various occasions and serve as a coordinator among the delegates and a liaison with conference managers from U. K. In our tours in the interior, in buses, the driver of the bus and perhaps another person as a guide, used to be with us, join us in lunch or dinner or tea, wherever we halted on the way. There was no distinction and they participated freely in all these, along with speakers and ministers.

In India, such things will be unthinkable. There was complete equality and they were treated as one of us. We visited the gold mines at Kalgoorli and saw how gold was extracted from a big lump of earth. We travelled in a fully air-conditioned train, (where every thing was provided), a distance of 1400 miles, in bush-country, saw their forests and how they were protected, including felling of huge trees, and measures to control forest fires. We lived in the train itself as there were no hotels to accommodate us — a big contingent of nearly 150 persons from the various Commonwealth countries. We used to have our breakfast, lunch and dinner in batches at convenient intervals.

In our entire delegation, there were quite a few blacks and the arrangements were that the leader of the delegation would have a whole compartment to himself, while others on a sharing basis, two in each compartment. Our delegates requested me to see that no black delegate shared their compartments. It was a shame to make such an atrocious suggestion, when we (Indians) were vociferous in condemning the practice of apartheid. We made such a big row, in Breach Candy, in Bombay, when Indians were prevented from entry into the baths, controlled by the whites who ran the club and the baths.

I have seen in these International Conferences, Whites mixing more freely with the Blacks than we ever did. Indians again formed a separate group of their own, and hardly mixed with other delegates. This is against the spirit of the Conference. While on tour in the interior, we visited a place called 'Mildura' near Sydney (New South Wales) where we were amazed to see an unending stretch of citrus plantation, with its luxuriant growth. We were told that the project was almost given up as there was no source of water to feed the plantation. But with persistent efforts, they were able to locate a source of water and hence this grand success.

When we visited Brisbane (Queensland) we were invited to a Govt. House Party by the Governor of the State. We went there in time — but the Governor was not to be seen. He came late. When questioned, they explained that this was a tropical country and nobody including the Governor kept the time. I was travelling in sports clothes, and they mistook me for the well-known cricketer from West Indies, Constantine. They were truly disappointed.

Raghunath Singh, M. P. was one of our delegates. He had brought special copper-plates, privately we thought, to be presented to each legislature of Australia. We arranged a special function at each place, for the ceremonial presentation. But the calculating M. P. sent his bill to Lok Sabha Secretary— covering the cost of the plates presented. When we were returning, leaving Canberra for Sydney, the plane developed some trouble. After reaching Sydney, at 4.30 p.m. we had to make a compulsory halt of nearly 6/8 hours before we took off. The Commander of the plane took us to Hotel Australia and arranged for our meals there. They took great care of us.

Australia is a big country — with a population of 10 million or so. It is mostly inhabited on the coastline, the interior being bush-country, barren and deserted. The original population of Aborigines is almost on the verge of extinction. Because of sparse population, they have introduced two very novel projects, Flying squad of Doctors to reach help wherever needed, quickly and Air Schools to teach children in different far-flung villages from a central place. The teacher used to call out the names of children on a roll-call and the children used to answer in like manner. It was very interesting to watch the whole thing. Atlee, the former P.M. of England, who was partly responsible for the grant of Independence to India, Sir Roland Michner, the Canadian Speaker of the House of Representatives, who later became the G. G. of Canada were among the delegates. We all used to breakfast, lunch, dinner together and we travelled in a common coach. We were like one big international family. We spent two months together like this. The last but not the least, was our trip to the underground thermal station at Tumat which was opened by Dame Menzies ..... wife of P. M. Menzies. Australia has not much of rainfall and there is a water problem.

In the scheme known as Snowy Mountain Scheme, they have pooled water from different sources and created a big reservoir of water, which was used for Hydro-Electric Power. We travelled in big Australian cars — 3 in each and all of us — 150 persons, were served tea, breakfast, lunch and dinner at the specified times, in systematic manner. In lunches and dinners, there used to be one waitress to cover six persons and everything was served hot and fresh, smoothly and with great efficiency.

There was a small function in Sydney to felicitate Atlee by the local Labour Party. Atlee was a sort of a self-effacing person and when asked to address the gathering, he rose and said just these few words, "Drink to the health of Labour" and sat down.

I had an occasion to escort Atlee from Govt. House to the Council Hall for a talk we had arranged, when he was passing through Bombay on his way to Ceylon. I have still, at this distance of time happy memories of the Conference. We had been to a hill-station by name *Whyalla*. They sold empty tins there, carrying precious hill-air in them. We saw in Adelaide, Capital of South Australia, a statue of a person standing with his finger pointing to the place, indicating that the town should be built there. We also saw the first airplane in a glass house, which touched Australia. These are very touching things.

In Australia, they have got what is known as a Temperance-Movement. Under this movement, public bodies especially hotels undertake not to serve liquor in their premises. India needs a movement like this instead of prohibition laws, which remain a dead letter. After return to India, I sent a report to the Lok Sabha secretariat, covering the Conference.

In 1965, I had an opportunity to attend the C.P.A. Conference in New Zealand. I have already mentioned elsewhere, how C. M. Vasantrao Naik wholeheartedly supported my visit. I left Bombay in a British plane on one afternoon — 12 noon to be exact. It was lunch time. When I told the air hostess that I was a vegetarian, she immediately improvised for me a vegetarian meal, though no vegetarian meals as such were provided in the plane. But with the resourceful attitude and help of the hostess, my purpose was served. I had no difficulty.

In this connection, I must mention my experience in an Indian Airlines plane, when I was going to Goa from Bombay for the Speaker's Conference. Though my office had taken care to inform the Indian Airlines, that I was a vegetarian, the air hostess blandly told me that vegetarian meal was not available since they had not been notified about it, which, of course, was not correct. The result was, I had to go without my meal.

After a halt at Sydney in Australia, we took off for Wellington (New Zealand), which is a further 1000 miles away from Australia and reached Wellington at about 7.30 P.M. in the evening. I had the impression that the plane was landing on the ground straight after coming over from the sea. Immediately I was received and escorted to my hotel 'Royal Oak'. As I was late in coming, I was asked to join other delegates, who had already proceeded on their tour at a certain place, the next day morning. So after a good night's rest in the hotel, I started the next day morning to join our other friends. There was another person, who was also late in coming to this country. He was one Asline, a delegate from Canada, and a parliamentary secretary in Federal Govt. of Canada. He was a young jolly person and we immediately became good friends. He was exceedingly social and free with every one. I kept company with him throughout my one month's stay in New Zealand. Soon, we two joined the other delegates.

New Zealand is a small country with hardly a population of 25 lakhs. It consists of two islands — North and South — islands. It is primarily an agricultural country. There is not much Industry. They have however created man-made forests, which is quite a success. Here also we are trying to do the same thing, which goes by the name of 'social forestry'. Morarjee Desai, who had come out of Govt. under Kamraj Plan, was the leader of the Indian delegation. Anjanabai Magar, MLA, was a delegate from Maharashtra. S. M. Krishna, then an MLA from Karnataka, now the C.M. of that State, was with us among others. He was a young sprightly boyish looking person and we became immediately good friends. Mallya was the other Secretary from Parliament, New Delhi. A. D. Mani, Editor of *The Hitawada,* Nagpur paper of the 'Servants of India Society' was also with us. I used to go to Nagpur for our Winter Sessions every year and our friendship was further strengthened and I had become their family friend. We were a good team and we worked smoothly for the Conference.

In the internal tours of the country, we visited places like Roturua, where we found hot springs and roses as big as dahlias, Milford Sound, a place of great scenic beauty, one watery cave, full of millions of glow worms emitting soft light, Christ-Church, a flourishing town, in the midst of the fertile valley of Canterbury, with its beautiful university, Auckland, another big town and last but not the least, a Maori settlement. Maoris are the original settlers of New Zealand who are quite fair in complexion but unlike the aborigines in Australia, it is a thriving community and the Govt. of New Zealand is trying to integrate them in the main stream of the population. Maori children and other European children were being educated in the same school together and given the same education, as one of the steps, for their integration.

Hanan, whom I had met in the Australian Conference as a delegate from New Zealand, was now a minister in his country. I think he was in charge of justice and Maoris. He was keen that persons settled in his country should be fully integrated in its population and not remain as a separate group. It seems that he did not like Indians going back to India and marrying Indian girls and then coming to their country. There is a sprinkling of Indian population, mostly Gujaratis from Navsari district of Gujarat, mainly engaged in vegetable business.

There was also, what was known as 'Chaurpague Cauldron' in Wairaker's awesome Geyser Valley, where all the varied thermal activities could be seen, with perfect ease. Another interesting thing was the geothermal power station, first in the Commonwealth and second in the whole world.

On our return, we stopped in Sydney (Australia) for a week at the invitation of the Australian Government, my second visit to that country.

Morarjee Desai, who was C. M. of Bombay for many years, then Finance Minister of Govt. of India and finally Deputy Prime Minister with Indira Gandhi as P. M., was the leader of the delegation. He never made any fuss about anything and he used to travel with us in the same coach wherever we went. He would be ready at the foyer exactly at 8 a.m. for joining us. Kanti Desai, his son, who had accompanied him, used to look after him. I knew Morarjeebhai in Bombay, as a State Legislature Secretary, fairly closely and I had no difficulty in carrying out my duties under his leadership.

We visited a place near Wellington — called Lower Hutt, where we witnessed children between 8-12 years, of age boys and girls riding their horses as trained horsemen. They were all expert in horse-riding and exhibited their skill before us. We were told that children were given horses for looking after them, doing everything to keep them properly, from washing, cleaning, brushing and feeding, etc. Children did that with great enthusiasm. We were told that, this, among other things prevented children from getting into mischief or going astray.

Commonwealth conferences serve a very useful purpose, providing a wonderful opportunity for the interchange of views between Commonwealth Parliamentarians on problems of mutual interests and concerns. Informal contacts made by members while on tour and during the conference period are invaluable. Normally, disputes between member-countries are not allowed to be brought up for discussion, though Pakistan always unsuccessfully tried to do so in regard to Kashmir problem.

I had also an opportunity to attend a UNESCO Conference on copyright matters in Paris, as the sole delegate of the Govt. of India, being a senior member of Indian Copyright Board. It was a unique experience. The signatory countries to the two world conventions in Copyright matters meet and discuss copyright problems in a forum of their representatives and try to arrive at common decisions, which are contained in the final joint resolution of the Conference. The signatory countries then are supposed to bring their copyright law in conformity with these recommendations.

Our Conference lasted for a week, everyday from 9 a.m. in the morning till 6 p.m. in the evening with tea/coffee and lunch breaks. It was a strenuous session, discussing the subject thoroughly. The problem we discussed was about the rights of the translators of the original books. Translations are a matter of great importance in Western countries, involving, as they do, translations of great classics and books on technical subjects. I think, the consensus was that the translators should have all the protection (as have the original authors) except as against the original authors. We slogged for a full week and produced a joint resolution. After the Conference, we were invited to a cocktail party given by the Assistant Secretary-General of the UNESCO organization. Our stay in Paris was enjoyable. I was staying in a hotel, in Duchane Avenue, just near the UNESCO building. Devarhubli, a relative of mine had married a French girl and settled in Paris. He and his family were of much assistance to me and I used to spend all my spare time with that family. The whole family had come to the airport to receive me and settle me in a nearby hotel in Duchane Avenue, after lunching with them. Paris is one of the most beautiful cities in the world. It has large avenues with rows of trees on either side. The big spacious road from Arc de Triumph to Place de Concord, a distance of nearly 2/3 kms with its footpaths on either side, as wide as our Marine Drive in Bombay, is one of the 18th century marvels. The hotels put their menus outside so that diners choose the hotels which serve dishes of their choice. There are footpath restaurants, people sit and sip coffee or beer etc. in a leisurely fashion. They are quite clean and orderly and perhaps a little cheaper.

After the Conference I went to London for a week. There was some gap in communication, with the result that there was no one to receive me at the airport or at the terminal and there was no way of contacting the concerned person, being a Saturday, a non-working day for them. There was a tourist assistant who was trying to help the travellers in the matter of hotel accommodation, transport, etc. I approached her with my requirements and she immediately fixed me in a convenient hotel in a suitable locality and instructed one of the taxi drivers to take me there. I was immediately driven to the specified hotel, where I was lodged in a convenient room. All these things happened without any fuss and quite smoothly. This was a real help. It was a nice hotel, 'Hyde Park' hotel, not far from the Parliament House, where I had work. The charges were 3 pounds a day with bed and breakfast. But while leaving the hotel they charged me only 70 shillings per day instead.

During my stay in London I contacted Robin Vanderfelt, Secretary-General of C.P.A. who arranged lunch for me and also fixed a breakfast appointment with the clerk of the House, Barnet, in his spacious accommodation of 16 rooms in the Parliament Building itself. When I went there on the appointed day, I was escorted by Mrs. Barnet and there I was introduced to another young officer of the House of Commons, whom Barnet described as the future Clerk of the House, at the turn of the century, that is, after 35 years or so. We had a nice talk, renewed old acquaintances and renewed the memory of my previous visit as a participant in the parliamentary course and things connected with it.

I also renewed my acquaintance with J. K. Ram, who had become my friend in India. I dined at his place one afternoon. His Swiss wife was very helpful and friendly and she helped me to do some shopping. After a week's stay I left for India. This was a very short stay abroad.

We were planning to build a new parliament house in Bombay. We, i.e. myself, Girme, Dy. Speaker,

Legislative Assembly and Jaywant the architect to the Govt., undertook an extensive tour in India, to see the parliament buildings wherever they had been newly constructed. Thus, we went to Chandigarh in Punjab, Bhuvaneshwar in Orissa, Bangalore in Karnataka, Calcutta in West Bengal and last but not the least, the parliament house in New Delhi. We found that the Delhi building was the best of all, complying with all the requirements of a parliament house. Meanwhile, I happened to read about the new parliament house in Kuala-Lumpur in Malaysia. I procured a copy of the blue print of the same, from S. V. Krishna Murthy Rao, Dy. Chairman of Rajya Sabha, who had gone there, for our use. Shankarrao Chavan, Minister for Buildings and Communication, was appraised of it. He suggested that we pay a visit to Kuala-Lumpur to see the building and gain first-hand knowledge about it.

Accordingly we — myself, Shankarrao and Jaywant, architect to the State Govt. went to Kuala-Lumpur and inspected the building. It was built on an extensive area of nearly 40 acres, with a huge banquet Hall and other things fully air-conditioned. In Bombay we had a plot of 1/2 acres to build the building. But eventually we adopted the same pattern. The new Council Hall in Bombay, which was opened by Prime Minister Indira Gandhi — follows closely the pattern of Kuala-Lumpur building. Jaywant, our architect, took great pains and spared no effort in planning the whole construction. We had stopped at Singapore on our way. We attended dinners both in Kuala-Lumpur and Singapore, official dinners, which were attended by diplomats and other high dignitaries of Govt. of the two places. The dinner at Kuala-Lumpur was under soft candle-lights. We visited also Bangkok on our return and saw the Buddha statues, reclining and emerald studded, and the floating market on Chou-Priya River. We were the guests of Air-India who looked after us. After about 2 days' halt, we returned to Bombay, by Air-India plane. On our onward journey we had stopped for 1/2 days in Ceylon and visited Kandy and other places.

Here I must also mention about my first visit to London, where I had gone for a parliamentary course, arranged by the British Branch of CPA for overseas parliamentarians and officers. It was of 2 months' duration and we had talks from knowledgeable persons everyday from 9 or 10 a.m. to 1 p.m. Sir Edward Fellows, Clerk of the House of Commons, Lidderdale, clerk Asst, Sir Patrick Spence, India's former Chief Justice of Federal Court, Gorden Walker, former Labour-Govt., Foreign Minister, Herbert Morrison and others lectured to us. After lectures, we used to have lunch in one of the dining-rooms of the Parliament House, (Westminster Palace) in the company of some prominent members and then attended the proceedings in the House. On my return to India, I introduced a similar course on parliamentary topics, which is still being held, at the instance of Y. B. Chavan, the then C.M.

The House of Commons chamber is a compact one, hardly sufficient for 300 persons — though the strength of the House is 625 or so. When the building was bombed during the war by German planes, it was rebuilt the same way, the same size. A big house is not convenient for parliamentary debates, where cut and thrust of speeches forms the main attraction.

I was lucky to watch the debate on the Suez Canal crisis. Aneuren Bevan, labour leader, was one of the principal speakers. He made a devastating speech on the inefficiency of Govt. He said that the Govt. had frittered away all the good things, prestige and good will, built by Labour Govt., by their wrong policies and governance. He thundered "England is founded on coal and surrounded by fish, yet there was shortage of both." He was truly a match for the great Churchill, the eminent conservative leader. Harold Macmillan, P. M. who had succeeded Anthony Eden, as England had lost face in the war against Egypt, replied. My stay in London was comfortable and fruitful. I was staying in Reubens Hotel near Buckingham palace and Charing-Cross hotel near Traffalgar Square. We watched the change of guards at 10, Downing Street and the trooping of the colours at White-Hall gate. Sir Howard De'guill, the Secretary General looked after me very well. I visited several places and clubs in his company.

We also visited Northern Ireland for a week. Northern Ireland was still with England. They sent their representatives to the House of Commons, as from one of the States in India, to Lok Sabha. There is serious cleavage of opinion, about severing British connection and joining the parent State, Irish Republic. They have their own parliament, known as 'Stormont House'. There is still no severance from Britain, though serious efforts are being made in that direction. Their constitution and working is like that of any one of our States.

For going to Belfast — Northern Ireland, we travelled in a train from Charing-Cross station to a certain port-town, reaching there at about 9 p.m. Dinner was served in the train. In the ship, I had a cabin for myself, luxuriously fitted. It was a fairly big luxury-liner. We arrived at Belfast the next morning, where we were received by the officers of the local parliament (N.Ireland). We were put up in a hotel at Bangor, a suburb of Belfast — a fine harbour town.

Irish linen is famous and I bought some. We had long evenings lasting till 9 p.m. After a week or so, we returned to London.

In our group there were Cherian, the then Chairman of Legislative Council, Madras and later the Governor of Maharashtra, and Mrs. Cherian, the former Mayor of Madras in her own right, Ismail, Speaker of the Ceylon-House of Representatives, among others. We also visited London County-Council and saw its working as also Kolchester County Council and its working.

Before I reached London, I had made convenient halts at Rome, Zurich, Geneva and Paris, lasting altogether for 2 weeks. In Rome and Paris, I was able to see their parliaments. My visit lasted a total of 2 and 1/2 months. After the course, I sought an opportunity to see the working of the Offices of the House of Commons. I introduced some of the things seen there in our Secretariat.

As for sightseeing, we went to the Tower of London, where we saw the King's jewels in a glass case, the place marked where Charles I, King of England, was beheaded, the long row of godowns on the bank of Thames River storing merchandise of the whole world, the mechanism of artificially raising the level of water to that of the godowns, to facilitate transport of stored goods and finally the parting of the tower bridge, to allow ships to pass through.

I had got very friendly with the Ceylon Speaker, who was very nice and we used to move together. When later, I went to Ceylon as a part of parliamentary tour, I was able to renew my old friendship and spend sometime with him at dinner. We visited Oxford-University town — very much urbanised unlike Cambridge. Stratford-upon-Avon — Shakespeare's place — Anne Hathaway's Cottage (his wife) as it was then, and the house which Shakespeare bought with the sale-deed still preserved. I bought a book — Complete works of Shakespeare — with the slip attached that it was bought from that place. In London, we saw 'Merchant of Venice', Shakespeare's play, in the old 'Vic Threatre' where only Shakespeare's plays are staged. We, myself and Dr. and Mrs. Cherian had breakfast with Vijayalaxmi Pandit, our High Commissioner in London at her residence, Kensington garden. London, a vast city, can still boast of a number of extensive parks in its midst, like Hyde Park, Kensington garden etc.

England is tradition-bound and the parliament still observes some of those old things like 'who goes there', 'Guy Fox, searching the cellar of H.C. with a lantern' etc. But they also follow policies and programmes developed through centuries. For example, they do not entertain any proposal to put up a portrait or a statue in its premises, until 5 years have elapsed after the death of that person. They do not make a reference in the House to any person who was not a Member of the House. The House is not adjourned unless it is on the death of serving P.M. We must follow these things. England, in its initial period has gone through a period of corruption. After election, the concern was chiefly who became a minister, rather than what he was going to do. England has now outlived that phase and today it is one of the most mature countries, relatively free from corruption and bad and irresponsible Govt. We can also hope that we will soon be free from corruption which today is all pervading, and experience good and efficient governance in future.

Chapter VII

MEN AND MATTERS IN LEGISLATURE

During a span of a quarter of a century I was the Secretary, M.L.S., for the first two decades and the remaining years as the First Secretary of Department of Legislative Affairs, which I had started and organized its working, I had come in close contact with my successive speakers of Legislative Assembly, Chairmen of Legislative Council and the Chief Ministers and the prominent members and I was able to observe their style of working at close quarters. I think it is necessary for me to put down my impressions about these great personalities.

When I first came to the Legislature, then known as B.L.D. (Bombay Legislative Department), D. K. Kunte was the Speaker and R. S. Hukerikar, the Chairman. Morarjee Desai was the Chief Minister. I have already described how I came to be appointed as Secretary of the Legislature. I had some initial difficulty to get along with Kunte, and but for the solid backing of Hukerikar and Morarjee Desai, it was well-nigh impossible for me to continue. But it seems that my stars were strong and I was able to steer through successfully and contribute solidly to the functioning of the Legislature in the following years — the earlier difficult 2/3 years notwithstanding.

I have already mentioned elsewhere about Kunte and my relations with him. R. S. Hukerikar was a nice man — a perfect gentleman and my rapport with him was excellent. He was also our family friend and I had very close relations with him. As the Chairman of Khadi Board, he sometimes held his office in my Foreshore bungalow No.8, where Vasudeo, our cook-cum-all-purposes-man, was always at his service, whether I was there or not. We had long and close association with him for many years till his death. In him we lost a good friend, guide and my benefactor. He was the Chairman of the Legislative Council for only one term and he earned a good name (Ajatshatru) in all sections of the House. He went back to Dharwar (Karnataka) after reorganization of States, and devoted himself completely to educational activities in Dharwar, where he built a big educational network comprising several disciplines.

Morarjee Desai was a tower of strength to me. He was always immaculately dressed in his kurta and pyjama and was ever available in the premises of the Council Hall when the Session was on. He did all his work — the work pertaining to his own department, himself, whether it was a bill, motions or questions. He answered a large number of questions, intricate and detailed by B. C. Kamble, to which I have already referred elsewhere. He was always present in the House, during the question hour which gave him an ample opportunity to watch the performance of his colleagues is answering questions. This is a good practice which deserves to be emulated by other ministers. This practice will enable them to see how the Departments of Govt. are functioning. He remained in the premises of Council Hall, till the end of the meeting and never failed to show up when the House rose for the day. He was honest and truthful to the core. His doors were always open to his partymen, because, he said, he owed his position to them. He was brutally frank, almost to a fault, which earned him many enemies. Here I may add that a person is a Chief Minister for the whole State and not only for his partymen even as a member elected to the Assembly from any constituency is a representative of the whole State, including the persons who have voted against him. This is because, election from a constituency is only a convenient method of choosing a person, to represent the whole State.

After Morarjee Desai's exit from the State and his elevation as Commerce Minister of Govt of India, in 1956, in the explosive situation following the S.M.S. Movement, Yeshwantrao Chavan came to be appointed as Chief Minister of Bombay. He was a junior member of Morarjee's cabinet, but because of Hiray's — (a senior Minister) — spearheading the movement of Samyukta Maharashtra with Bombay city in direct opposition to Morarjee's views, Yeshwantrao, was the natural and obvious choice. Yeshwantraoji was the product of the stormy times, particularly a product of the political crisis generated by the powerful movement for S.M. in the forties and the fifties. Every crisis throws up a leadership which meets the situation. The leadership here came in the shape of Yeshwantraoji. He was the first Chief Minister of bigger bilingual State including Gujarat, Vidarbha and Marathwada. He had a difficult and delicate task as the movement for S.M. was at its height and the Congress rule in the State was sustained by the Vidarbha element in the Congress. After the bigger bilingual State of Bombay was split into two unilingual States of Maharashtra and Gujarat in 1960 he was again the Chief Minister of Maharashtra, the first Chief Minister of Samyukta Maharashtra. Coming as he did after Morarjee Desai, one cannot resist the temptation of contrasting the two personalities who were so different from one another. Morarjeebhai was rigid and uncompromising, but not so Yeshwantraoji who was flexible and accommodating. One was aggressive in approach, while the other was conciliatory. One was intolerant of the opposition, while the other was tolerant and cared for the opposition's views. Barring these differences one can say that both were disciplined, diligent in their work, respected the parliamentary norms and traditions, and took keen interest in the proceedings.

Morarjee was first opposed to the formation of a bigger bilingual State, as he feared that it would be split into two unilingual States of Maharashtra and Gujarat, a prophecy, which came true, within a short time. But he was true to his word and never did anything to undo the bilingual State despite the pressure from Gujarat.

Chavan was a good administrator who successfully steered the State during those difficult days. But he was different. He quietly worked for the formation of Maharashtra. Jivraj Mehta hinted at it, as much, when he observed that they (Gujarat) were driven out. It has, however, always appeared, to be an enigma to me that Yeshwantraoji, a product of Morarjee's creation, never worked and sided with Morarjee particularly when his help was needed. Morarjee's Govt. under Janata Party in Delhi, would not have fallen if Yeshwantraoji had gone to his rescue. I also cannot help feeling that Morarjee would have been a great support to Indira Gandhi, then Prime Minister, if she had not thrown him out, exercising her prerogative as she thought, as the Prime Minister. It must be remembered that Indira Gandhi became the Prime Minister as a compromise. P. M. Kamraj and the Congress Party generally agreed to support Indira Gandhi for Prime Ministership provided she agreed to Morarjeebhai's inclusion as the Dy. Prime Minister. This had to be done because, Morarjee was bent on fighting the election. But we do not know what were the political compulsions of Indira Gandhi for acting the way she did. Perhaps she trusted no one. She had agreed to this. How then could she throw him out in that fashion. However, no one raised this question. Again, Morarjee would have been an excellent Prime Minister if he had not been obdurate and had not shown excessive love for his son Kanti who brought him a bad name. Morarjee seemed to be a person, persona-non-grata with Maharashtra. May be because of his views on Samyukta Maharashtra and the strong action he took against the agitators. But even otherwise, Marathi press was, on the whole, anti-Morarjee. He was not anti-Maharashtra at all. He spoke excellent Marathi. He loved Maharashtra. But for no reason, the Marathi press called him names and created an impression that he was against Maharashtra. I always thought that he was unjustly treated.

Vasantrao Naik was our Chief Minister for over 10 years. He was to succeed immediately Y. B. Chavan who went to Delhi as Defence Minister. But Kannamwar from Vidarbha was a more powerful candidate, who could not be passed over. Anyway Kannamwar's regime was short due to his untimely and premature demise. V. P. Naik became the Chief Minister. He was basically a cultured gentleman with a broad mind. He was always sympathetic towards people and tried to help them as far as possible. He was polite and never uttered a harsh word against any one. He was equally popular with his partymen as with those of the opposition. This made his task easy in carrying out his work, whether inside or outside the Legislature. There were explosive issues like FEDCO and Nanavati. In the FEDCO case, the directors of the company who had been convicted and sentenced by a competent court were released by the Govt. on grounds which did not seem convincing. Likewise the Govt. had no proper answer when Nanavati, the Naval Officer was released from jail by the Governor exercising his prerogative. This action also did not seem to satisfy the public. But both the matters passed off smoothly, Govt. shortcomings notwithstanding. This was due to the personality of Vasantrao Naik, whom nobody wanted to offend. He was a good manager of persons and things. He had tremendous patience. Yeshwantrao Chavan once described Vasantrao as a person sitting patiently with a fishing rod in his hand and a pipe in his mouth till he was able to strike, successfully. He was Ajatashatru. Elsewhere I have mentioned his many kindnesses to me personally. When I went to thank him with my wife, for giving a palatial flat to me despite opposition from the Chief Secretary, he was gracious enough to receive us with his wife and told me in flattering words that I fully deserved it. Even, when in a conference, I was criticized in a manner to poison his mind against me, he maintained his equanimity and refused to be influenced by any such things.

When Goa Assembly passed a resolution to merge Goa in Maharashtra, we had called a morning session to accept the offer of merger. The Govt. had made lavish arrangements for publicity. They had wanted to take photographs in the Assembly Hall for which they had made arrangements. When I noticed this, I spoke to the Speaker Bharade, that these things were not permissible under our established practice and he rang Vasantrao Naik, that this should be stopped. Vasantrao immediately agreed to do so, to the great chagrin and disappointment of the Chief Secretary specially, who even indirectly hinted that Govt. would not take this lying down and would deal with me and my Secretariat accordingly. Of course, we did not attach much importance to that, being independent of them. His untimely death was a great loss to the State and the country, generally.

S. K. Wankhede became our Speaker in 1972 and continued in that office till 1977. He was a member of the Legislative Assembly, Member of Parliament, right from 1952 to 1979. His parliamentary career began from 1939. He had held various important offices such as the Chairman of the Nagpur District Council and Mayor of Nagpur Municipal Corporation, which office he held continuously for 3 years among other things. He was first Dy. Speaker of Madhya Pradesh Legislative Assembly in 1952 and after re-organisation of States he again became Dy. Speaker of the Bombay Legislative Assembly. Thereafter he became a Minister of Bombay Govt. He continued as Minister, holding various portfolios — particularly the Finance portfolio. I had known him, right from the time he was Dy. Speaker of Madhya Pradesh Legislative Assembly. We used to meet year after year at the time of presiding officers' conference. Wankhede will be remembered as an extremely amiable and social person endowed with qualities of head and heart. He had no prejudice of any kind and would mix freely with all without any sense of superiority. He had an innate sense of humour, which helped him greatly in the conduct of proceedings in the Assembly. He did everything with grace and left his impress in whatever he did. He had great respect for the House and its procedure.

My relations with him as a Minister of Finance were not quite happy. Somehow he thought that I was creating trouble for him, in the matter of financial business whether it was the annual budget or supplementary demands. I was doing nothing of the kind. I used to read the papers in that connection carefully, and locate the flaws, if any, so that I could advise the Speaker, if the need arose. I also used to alert the Govt. on those things so that they could be ready to answer, if necessary. This seems to have created some misunderstanding in his mind. I never tried to correct his impression in the matter, since I had done no such thing and also because it might have sent a wrong signal. When he came as a speaker I decided to quit after my term — I was already under extension for several years — because of my experience with him as a Finance Minister. But to my great surprise, Wankhede would not allow me to go and he ensured for me further extension, by personally approaching the concerned Ministers and the C.M. during the session. He must have realised that I was not at fault. It was a rare gesture on his part. He died suddenly of heart attack in 1988 and we lost in him a good and amiable friend.

Sharad Pawar was the Chief Minister during the period from 18th July 1978 to 16th Feb. 1980. He became C. M. under rather unusual circumstances. The Congress had been returned in the election in 1977 with no decisive majority. It had two factions, one led by Vasantdada Patil and the other by Nasikrao Tirpude which was Indira Congress. The two factions of the Congress had fought the election against each other. But after the election, they came together to form a Govt. with the help of a few independents. They succeeded in forming a Govt. with Vasantdada Patil as the C.M. Shivraj Patil was the Speaker. But there was no love lost between the two factions. A game of defections from the other faction had started to swell its own number. In these circumstances Pawar decided to leave the coalition with a sizable number of 50 or so members reducing Vasantdada Patil's ministry to a minority and join hands with the Janata Party. They formed a coalition known as Progressive Democratic Front and Pawar headed the coalition and thus became the Chief Minister. The Govt. was however abruptly dismissed by P. M. Indira Gandhi, for no rhyme or reason. His regime however as the Chief Minister was quite promising and the coalition Govt. was working smoothly and successfully.

Pawar is a young dynamic person, full of promise. He is well-educated and well-versed in Marathi, Hindi and English. He has widely travelled visiting several countries abroad. He is a mass leader and has worked his way up from the grassroots level. Recently, he has again broken away from the Congress on the grounds of foreign origin of Sonia Gandhi, the Congress President, projected as its Prime Minister. He has again repeated the earlier experiment and joined hands with the Congress to form the Govt. in Maharashtra. When he had headed the coalition Govt. earlier, I had worked with him as a Parliamentary Advisor.

In our crusade to reform our procedure wholesale, to bring it in tune with the Constitutional requirements, to Silam, our Speaker, belongs the lion's share of credit. We carried out a series of reforms towards this end, and Silam gave great support and encouragement. He was a very senior politician and was therefore in a position to put across our case to the Govt. frankly and fearlessly. Our methodology was simple. We used to prepare our case foolproof from all sides and put it to the Govt. at the Secretary's level. It used to be rejected as expected. Then we would take up the matter at a ministerial level, where we invariably succeeded. This was a delicate and difficult process, spread over a long time. But we had enough patience. So we succeeded in our mission. Silam would call me a number of times to get convinced about any matter, but after he was convinced, he would not budge. He would even accept my advice against the Advocate-General's. He was a towering personality and he conducted the proceedings of the House with great dignity. The opposition was very strong in the wake of S. M. movement but we were able to manage the House skilfully with tact and patience. For this purpose, we recognized the opposition parties officially and they elected their leaders by rotation. It was a smooth affair. I had complete rapport with him and he trusted me fully. He was also very correct in his conduct and dealings. When we went to Delhi for official work, and we did so frequently, he never charged the Govt. more than absolutely necessary. There was a little gap between the time when he ceased to be the Speaker, and again re-elected after general elections, he handed over the Govt. car and the keys to me, during that interregnum. After his retirement from Speakership, he was appointed as Lt. Governor of Pondicherry. I visited Pondicherry with my wife and we were treated with great love and affection. There was an art school in Pune under his patronage, as its founder, and the students had prepared his portrait and offered it to us for display in the Council Hall. We accepted the offer. I was able to render this service to him, for his great services to the Legislature, with the tactful help and cooperation of Chief Minister, Vasantrao Naik, despite some opposition from some quarters.

We had started a 'Parliamentary Journal for Information', as one of our activities, in the Secretariat. It was quite successful, through our joint efforts. Thorat, our Librarian and Information officer, took great pains to produce the journal of quality and excellence. After I left, the journal ceased to be produced, after a few issues. It requires dedicated services from knowledgeable persons, to produce a journal of this kind. It is regrettable that this service is no longer available now. Even now, it is not too late to restart it. I was openly complimented by late P. V. Gadgil, a veteran journalist for the excellent quality of the journal and especially for 'my review' of the report on 'The Centre-States relations' by Raj Manner, former Chief Justice of Madras.

The process of procedural reforms started in Silam's time was continued further under T. S. Bharade, who became the new Speaker. Bharade adorned the chair for two terms i.e. 10 years. In the second term, his election was unanimous. He was adept in conducting the proceedings. His grasp of the subject was something bordering on the fabulous. At times, he used to come to the House almost a few minutes before its commencement. But within that short time, he would grasp everything and conduct the meeting in such a way as if he had been fully briefed about all the matters coming before the House. He had an excellent temper and temperament which helped him do everything coolly and effortlessly. At times, the House used to be in a turmoil. But he never lost his cool. He did not allow himself to be provoked, even when the provocation was great. Such provocation was frequently given by Jambuwantrao Dhote, who observed no norms and did not seem to respect the Chair, much. Bharade bore it patiently and seemed to ignore whatever Dhote said. Dhote had been punished by the House for contempt, by terminating his membership. He was re-elected from the same constituency. When this was pointed out by Dhote, in a triumphant tone, Bharade observed that his termination of membership and as also his re-election were both in accordance with the rules and established practice. He was adept in coining apt Marathi words for English expressions like 'प्रश्नमाला' for question-list or प्रश्नवेला for question-hour or भूक्षेप for floor crossing etc. Once the use of भूक्षेप had caused an amusing situation. Acharya Dandekar from Vidarbha had crossed the floor, meaning, he had passed, in the House, through the line connecting the Speaker and the Member speaking, and Bharade observed that the Hon. Member should desist from doing that (In Marathi भूक्षेप करु नये). The reporter had written down अंगविक्षेप करु नये meaning that the Hon. Member should not indulge in making unseemly gestures. The member promptly complained about this, and the matter was set right by correcting the script, amidst laughter.

Bharade had a great sense of humour and used to make apt witty remarks, to put the House in good humour. The House proceedings would hear this out especially during the question hour.

Once there was an occasion to give a ruling on the admissibility of the demands for grants. The point was that these demands had been voted once and they were brought up for a second time, for voting, as the Departments concerned had been reorganised, in the matter of those services. The demands were thus not in order. Demands for grants are made for services and not for departments. Whoever renders that service would get that grant.

There was a lot of discussion with the Finance Secretary Damry who argued the point strenuously and persistently. An elaborate ruling was prepared as to why we considered the 'demands' out of order. Ultimately it was agreed on our suggestion, that the Finance Minister Wankhede, should not move the 'demands' for sanction saying that it was proposed under some misapprehension. Girme, the Deputy Speaker, requested Bharade that he should be allowed to take the Chair and give this important ruling. Bharade graciously agreed. But in the meanwhile, Page, the Chairman of the Legislative Council, gave the ruling prepared by us, when the matter came before that House. Legislative Council only discusses the demands but does not vote on them. Even so, Page gave the ruling to the utter discomfiture of Girme, and Page earned big headlines in the press the next day. My rapport with him (Bharade) was complete and he had hardly any occasion to differ from me. He was a simple man, unassuming in the extreme. His addresses while inaugurating the 'Assurances Committee' meeting or opening the parliamentary course for University students were memorable and showed deep insight into those subjects. He was a great authority in Sant literature and would conduct discussions on it and perform even Kirtans during his tenure of Speakership. I have already adverted to his memorable speech on the Condolence Resolution on the demise of Pandit Nehru in the House.

I must also refer to his most apt observations in the following two cases. Some person from Ahmednagar had approached him for securing admission for his son in a medical college. Though the boy had scored very high marks, he could not be admitted because he was under age. Bharade said that even 'ज्ञानेश्वर' an intellectual prodigy could not have been admitted in any university here because of under age. In another case, he observed that — now-a-days the political aspirants prefer like 'गणपती', or 'गौतमऋषी' to do perambulation (go round his parents or a cow as the case may be) round some political heavyweight, rather than do the more important thing, viz. doing some significant service to the people or nursing the constituency.

When Bharade finally announced his retirement, after the end of his term, I arranged the proceedings exactly in the way it is done in H.C. in England. It is something like a ceremony. Ceremony is an integral part of the parliamentary procedure.

When Churchill, Britain's P. M., retired, there was an interesting proceeding in that connection. The House appointed a committee of the representatives of the two parties, to draft a suitable resolution, which was moved and several members spoke on it eulogizing the services rendered by the great man. The committee waited upon Churchill at his residence and handed over to him the resolution and the proceedings thereon. Thereupon Churchill made a suitable reply to it, which was reported back to the House in a ceremonial manner.

V. S. Page was the Chairman of the Legislative Council during the same period. Page was equally scholarly and deep in the studies of Sant literature, among other things. He had the longest tenure of 18 years — 3 terms of 6 years each. Kharabe, the additional Secretary, was in charge of Council work and proceedings. In difficult situations, I used to help him and get the things sorted out. Page was talented and conducted the proceedings ably. He also chaired important committees appointed by the Lok Sabha. But basically he was a politician and somewhat unpredictable. He was one of the mentors of the Congress Party. His contribution in some of the things like 'Employment Guarantee Scheme' and 'cause of the freedom fighters' was valuable. He was greatly respected in the Congress circles. He was a true Gandhian and even wanted to introduce 'walkouts and धरणे' (persistent and determined sitting before the authorities for a cause) in the rules of procedure. He was however quite simple and unassuming. He took me once to a circus show in Bombay, saying that he knew those people, who were mostly from Tasgaon, from where he hailed. I had no difficulty in getting along with him and he used to accept the suggestions made by me. All in all, I had a very happy and fruitful time during the regime of Page and Bharade.

I was commissioned by the Speaker Shankarrao Jagtap to prepare a commemorative volume, on the completion of 50 years of the Legislative Assembly. I accepted the offer with some hesitation, but was able to do the job, with my determination and the active support of the Speaker. The volume was released at a special function in Nagpur. I was presented by S. D. Sharma, then the Vice President of India, with a silver and gold plated plaque containing pictures of the Legislature buildings in Bombay, Pune and Nagpur and some gifts. It was a grand function, attended by high dignitaries including Chandrachud, the former

Chief Justice of the Supreme Court. I attended with my wife Padmavati.

During our stay in Nagpur, we were able to renew our friendship with Kanchanmala Raje Bhonsale, Rani-Saheb of Nagpur, who had distanced herself away from us for some time due to some strained relations between the two cousins Nirmala Raje Bhosale and Kanchanmala Raje. This was a matter of great satisfaction to us.

When I finally retired and relinquished charge from the Legislature, there were proceedings in both the Legislative Assembly and the Legislative Council in 1973 in appreciation of my services to the Legislature. The proceedings started on the basis of my identical letters addressed to the Chairman, Legislative Council and Speaker, Legislative Assembly in that connection (See appendix III). There were appreciating speeches paying tributes to me both by the Treasury Benches and the opposition members (Chief Minister Vasantrao Naik, D. B. Patil, Mrinal Gore and Mhalgi in Legislative Assembly and Vasantdada Patil, Minister for Irrigation, U. L. Patil, Maniben Patel, in Legislative Council) and finally followed by suitable observations by the Speaker Wankhede and the Dy Chairman, R. S. Gavai. I was gratified and overwhelmed to find such goodwill and good opinion about me and my services and I felt that my services were amply rewarded. (See proceedings ... Sept. 1973 Appendix IV)

Shivraj Patil was the Speaker during 1978-79. He was highly qualified having obtained the degrees of B. Sc. and LL.M. of the Bombay University. He was studious and painstaking in whatever he did. His rulings were therefore marked by deep study and knowledge of parliamentary procedure and practice.

Later he chose to enter a wider field in Delhi, where after becoming a minister of state for a few years, he was elected to the office of Speaker of Lok Sabha. Whether in Bombay or Delhi he made his mark as an able speaker, conducting the proceedings with poise, dignity and decorum. His rulings on difficult and delicate questions were always marked by deep study, and learning which he brought to bear on them. However, some of his rulings were controversial. I would refer to his rulings on the question of 'subjudice', in Bombay and defection of members in Delhi, as specific instances, in this connection.

He was always well-dressed. In his behaviour, whether in the House or outside, he was uniformly polite and courteous, marked by suave manners. He did me a great honour by remaining present throughout when I spoke on parliamentary privileges, to the university students. I also cannot forget his disappointment at being unable to secure general agreement for starting an 'Institute of Constitutional and Parliamentary Studies and Practice', which he very much desired.

Shankarrao Jagtap became the Speaker of the Assembly in 1985, after a short stint as a Dy. Speaker. His rise to his position was rapid, in less than 8 years since he was elected as a member. Before that, he had been a member of Public Accounts Committee and Estimates Committee also.

In the house he conducted himself with poise and dignity. He allowed members sufficient freedom to express themselves on matters that came up before the House and hardly interfered in that. He was popular with all sections of the House, including the opposition members although he had to face several piquant situations calling for great tact, ability and skill of management. He took time for taking decisions because of his anxiety to consider the matter in all its aspects.

His greatest contribution to the Institution was his signal success in arranging the Golden Jubilee Celebrations of Maharashtra Legislative Assembly on a grand scale — the inaugural session of which was opened by late Prime Minister Rajiv Gandhi. He undertook a number of schemes in connection with these celebrations, such as bringing out a number of publications useful to the members and the public alike, an exhibition highlighting the developments in the State insofar as the Assembly was concerned, and arranging a number of seminars and symposia on parliamentary and constitutional matters. In this he worked very hard, personally and was also able to secure help and cooperation from every section of the House as also of the concerned departments of Government. This speaks volumes for his tact and organizing capacity for arranging all these things on a big scale.

I am particularly beholden to him for asking me to prepare a commemorating volume, covering 50 years of Maharashtra Legislative Assembly (1937-87) to mark its Golden Jubilee. I am glad to say that I was able to accomplish this task successfully, with his ready help and cooperation, in every way. He personally took interest in seeing that the volume was brought out in the best possible manner, whether its printing or its good get-up. I wish that it had been a priced publication, in which case, it would have had a wider recognition. It was however unfortunate that his relations either with the Secretary, Bhaskar Shetye, my successor, (not immediate) or his colleague

Jayantrao Tilak, the chairman of Legislative Council were not happy.

I had no such experience in my long career of 20 years and I am proud to say that the Speakers Silam and Bharade carried on excellently with Page. I think that much depends on the Secretaries working with them. Jayantrao Tilak did not seem to like my agreeing to accept the assignment of the preparation of the golden jubilee volume which perhaps was coloured by his relations with the Speaker, a sort of transferred epithet, so to say. I however had told him that I would have equally accepted his assignment as well, if any.

Before I conclude on presiding officers, I must make a brief mention about K. T. Girme, who was our Dy. Speaker for two terms i.e. 10 years. He deserved to be elevated to the office of Speakership, because of his study of the Constitution and parliamentary procedure and practice. Earlier, in Pune, he had made a name in Municipal politics. It attracted the notice of Yeshwantrao Chavan, who brought him to the State Legislature. But he seemed to have stopped there and did not go to its logical end viz. see him elevated to the high office of Speakership.

Girme was studious. He devoted considerable time to peruse parliamentary literature, proceedings, books, etc. Occasionally he used to take part in the debates in the House. I remember his having taken part in the discussion of 'River Water Dispute'. There is an Act of Parliament on this subject which he cited and pleaded to solve the question on that basis. He has written a book in Marathi on parliamentary procedure and practice, especially with reference to the Maharashtra Legislature. It was well received in public. He was naturally disappointed at being denied the highest post. He used to be the Chairman of the 'Committee on Petitions' ex-officio and he did valuable work there. He died a premature death, a few years ago.

Of the opposition members, I propose to deal with K. N. Dhulup and G. A. Deshmukh (P.W.P.), Mrinal Gore and Bapusaheb Kaldate (Socialists), Mhalgi and Hashu Advani (B.J.P.) and A. B. Bardhan (C.P.I.).

K. N. Dhulup, began with considerable diffidence in the early stages — but with years, he developed confidence and maturity and ended as a successful leader of the opposition. As the leader of the opposition he had the privilege to open the attack during the discussion of the Governor's address and general discussion on the budget. He used to make preparations, as he himself said once, days and even months in advance. His preparations consisted in noting carefully the ministerial utterances on various occasions, and making skilful use of the same. He was once criticized for being a member of the Police Commission, to which he rejoined by emphatically asserting that he cared very little for that membership and it would, in no way affect his role of the opposition which he would fulfil to the hilt. Privately he was a simple and unassuming man and was quite popular with all sections of the House.

G. A. Deshmukh, a very senior member and now probably with his recent election he might be the senior-most member of the Assembly. He has no oratorical skill. He would perform duties as a representative of the people with courage of conviction and sincerity of purpose. He is being returned to the Assembly from the same constituency, term after term, which speaks volumes for the constructive work, which he is doing there. He is extremely simple and unassuming. He had adorned the office of a Minister during the rule of Progressive Democratic Front under Chief Minister Sharad Pawar and now again under Vilasrao Deshmukh. He is one of the few persons remaining true to his ideology and serving people unostentatiously.

Mrinal Gore was a stormy petrel of the opposition. Before she came to the Assembly, she did considerable work in the Bombay Corporation. She was feared and respected. She used to make careful preparations by actually visiting the places and gathering first-hand information. This gave her great advantage which enabled her to speak with authority. When she rose to speak, the Treasury Benches used to be in jitters, as she would, without fear or favour, lay bare the misdoings of Ministers in administration. She had a clean record of public life, and her personal life was without any blemish. It was for this reason that she was chosen to lead the attack on a 'no confidence motion' against Vasantrao Patil's ministry.

She had consulted me about the form of the 'no confidence motion'. I had told her that there are two forms for the purpose. One was a simple one-line motion i.e. this House has no confidence in the Council of Ministers reasons for that being supplied to Govt. separately, so as to enable them to reply. This form is convenient when there is multiplicity of the opposition parties, especially when they do not speak with one voice and at times even at cross purposes. The other form is meant to focus attention of the House on one or two specific issues, which are incorporated in the motion itself, to censure the Govt. and demand resignation on that basis. Mrinal Gore eventually adopted the one-line-Motion, after consulting her colleagues. I personally thought that they should have chosen 'Issue Based Motion' because there was available such an issue at that time to form the main ground of attack. She was one of the prominent members of the opposition and she functioned with great success.

Kaldate was a speaker par-excellence. He had a great gift of the gab which he used effectively as a member of the opposition. He spoke Marathi and Hindi equally well. When he rose to speak especially in the discussion on Governor's address or general discussion on the Budget, Yashwantrao used to make it a point to attend specially to hear him. I had an excellent rapport with him and we were good friends. Now he has become a member of Rajya Sabha and is functioning on an all India-plane. Socialists have by and large, clean public records. They still appeal to certain sections of the people. Personally I think, socialism is a spent force. It had its value once but with its limited appeal being fulfilled and the ruling party itself adopting some of their policies and programmes, their "raison-d'etre" has come to an end. Even in England, Labour Party has lost much of its value and utility, and they could form their Govt. after a gap of 15 years or so, for a change. Now the Labour Party has been adopting conservative policies, and that is why they are expected to last.

Mhalgi belonged to Jana-Sangha and its new version B.J.P. He spoke excellent Marathi and although they formed a small party, they made their impact by study of the subjects under discussion and procedural niceties. He was elected to be a member of Lok Sabha and there also he did his work efficiently and in a very systematic manner. He used to maintain regular files about his parliamentary work, to which he devoted considerable time and energy. In recognition of his work the party has instituted 'Mhalgi Pratishthan' under the auspices of which a lot of work is being done to strengthen democracy. His untimely death has removed from our midst an able and sincere parliamentarian. Once he spent the whole night in strenuously moving amendment after amendment to a certain Bill and spoke on them. Mhalgi would surely have been a minister now, in the B.J.P.-led Govt. at the centre.

Hashu Advani also of B.J.P. was mainly an effective organiser and a great constructive worker. He has created a strong network of organizations for various purposes in Chembur where he lived and functioned. He was studious and knew very well the niceties of the Parliamentary game. His expression was poor and that made it sometimes difficult to follow, what he wanted to say. But he had valid points which was the result of his study and ground-level work. He was a minister for sometime under Janata rule and I am sure he did his work very well. He was simple and unassuming and had a clean public record personally. He died recently thus removing another parliamentarian of note.

A. B. Bardhan of C.P.I. was an excellent parliamentarian. He was our member for one or two terms. He spoke excellent English, Hindi, and Marathi. Yashwantrao Chavan paid him open tributes for his qualities of head and heart. In the case of an official Bill proposing inclusion of certain areas in Nagpur Corporation limits, he pointed a lacuna which went to the root of the matter and the Govt. had to withdraw the bill. He respected the House procedure and of course, the Chair. He is now the General Secretary of C.P.I. where he is functioning effectively.

G. P. Pradhan was a member of the Legislative Council and was for some time the leader of the opposition there. He was one of the prominent members and was known for his suave manners and reasonable approach in all matters which came before the House. He was respected by both the Treasury and the Opposition alike. He is still active in public life. He studied his briefs carefully and put across his views in a lucid manner. He spoke English and Marathi equally well.

Of the lady members, I would like to say a few things about Nirmala Raje Bhonsale, Pratibha Patil, Prabha Rao, Anjanabai Magar, Vimal Rangnekar and Prabhavati Zadbuke (all Congress). I have already dealt with Mrinal Gore as an opposition Leader. Nirmala Raje Bhonsale, Ranisaheb of Akkalkot was our Parliamentary Secretary during Morarjee's time. Then she rose to be in due course, Dy. Minister and Minister. She had an attractive and impressive personality. She was always immaculately dressed and had a bearing and manners and grace, worthy of a royal family to which she belonged. She was intelligent and her performance in the House was quite adequate, though it could have been better, if she had taken more interest in the proceedings. She had an aura of her own and was not easily approachable.

My wife and I had close relations with her. We were family friends. During Nagpur Sessions, we, along with Kanchanmala Bhonsale, her first cousin, Rani Saheb of Nagpur, spent most of our spare time together with lunches and dinners in the Bhonsale Palace, seeing pictures and other places of entertainment. She had an excellent library at home and I used to regularly borrow books from her. Sharada Mukherjee was another member of our small group. We used to meet periodically and have luncheons and dinners together. Last days of Nirmala Raje were bordering on the pathetic. She led a lonely life and probably suffered from it. We tried to persuade Sharada Mukherjee and her brother to take care and look after her. But they were also not in a position to do much in that regard. Eventually, we succeeded in prevailing upon Kanchanmala to come and look after her which she did sincerely and assiduously. When she died, we did the funeral services. It was somewhat tragic that she, who was the grand niece of Sayajirao Gaekwad of Baroda and Rani-Saheb of Akkalkot, and later on minister of Govt. had to end her days in that way. But destiny is destiny. Nobody, great or small can escape it.

Pratibha Patil, a highly qualified person, was one of our prominent members, who took part in various debates, and gave good speeches. She was very ambitious. She became a Minister in due course and functioned effectively as such. She even rose to be the Deputy Chairman of Rajya Sabha, where she discharged her functions with dignity, poise and efficiency. She had also cast her eyes on the covetous post of C.M. but that did not come to pass. She even functioned as the leader of the opposition during the Janata rule, with the same efficiency and ability.

Prabha Rao was another lady member who was dynamic and somewhat aggressive in nature. She spoke excellent Marathi. She was our Minister for some time. She discharged her functions effectively and with a degree of firmness. It was alleged that her husband interfered in her work as a minister, which of course, she flatly and firmly denied. She has recently been elected to be a member of Lok Sabha.

Anjanabai Magar was another lady member of importance. She spoke well and took part in various debates in the House. She was a good social worker and had adorned the position of the Chairman of 'Children's Aid Society'. She was a delegate to the CPA Conference in New Zealand which I also attended as the Secretary of the delegation. She spoke in the open house fairly well in English, though she was not quite used to it. She was a nice person to get along with.

Vimal Rangnekar was active as a member. She used to bring matters before the House, on various subjects, made good preparations, spoke well and did her duties, on the whole with care and attention. She was social and friendly.

Prabhavati Zadbuke was a dynamic young lady. She did not take much part in the House proceedings. But when she did, she made a mark. She was a good speaker; she spoke excellent chaste Marathi with force and a certain measure of aggressiveness.

Chapter VIII
LEGISLATIVE REFORMS AND A FEW SUGGESTIONS

In the matter of procedure, the Parliament in Delhi has introduced or tolerated for some reasons, the practice of zero hour, which has no sanction in our rules of procedure or anywhere else in the parliaments of the world. It begins without there being any provisions for it after the question hour, and goes on, as long as for 30, 40, 50 minutes or so, when members raise questions, which they think are important, obliging the concerned minister to reply. Now the minister has no notice of the matter — he is in no position to give an authentic reply — the member also has probably raised the matter based on newspaper reports which are by no means authentic and sometimes may be also motivated. The Speaker also seems to be helpless in not being able to stop it. Speakers have, however, tried to limit such discussions to not more than half an hour. But this is neither here or there. I understand that even the Lok Sabha's daily bulletin starts with disapproval of such methods. Rajya Sabha on the contrary, seems to welcome it, probably because it must oppose what Lok Sabha does.

The practice which has been in vogue for quite some time should be stopped at once. It is completely contrary to parliamentary procedure and practice, since matters have to be brought before Parliament with a proper notice and also they require the Speaker's permission. Besides, such discussions are fruitless and they serve no purpose, except giving some undeserved publicity to the member. Fortunately, the evil has not spread to the States and I hope that the Speaker of Lok Sabha will show sufficient courage and firmness to stop this unparliamentary practice. Perhaps it would be better to do so by persuading the members to agree to it.

The other question which I wish to mention is about the new prevalent practice of moving 'Confidence Motions'. There is no specific provision in the rules of procedure to move a Motion of Confidence in the ministry, as there is for 'a no confidence motion'. Whoever has started this practice, has done no good to parliament. A 'Motion of Confidence' in the ministry is brought under a general rule, governing motions which are used for any matter of public importance, including the question of confidence. It is not illegal, like the zero hour, but is contrary to parliamentary practice and procedure. Such motions are generally brought when directed by the Governor or the President as the case may be, who also stipulates that it should be done in a particular time — which varies according to the circumstances — political, I may add. The procedure for 'no confidence motions' is fixed under the rules of procedures and the control of the whole thing from the beginning to the end is exercised by the Speaker and the House, unlike in the case where the President/Governor directs. For both these reasons, this practice should be stopped forthwith. It is followed nowhere else in the parliamentary world. I also cannot help feeling like many others that

Vajpayee Govt. would not have fallen with the withdrawal of support of A.I.D.M.K. members of Jayalalitha — if the opposition had moved a 'No Confidence Motion' as it should have, in the House, which was in session, and so saved the nation from a precipitate general elections, costing hundreds of crores of rupees to the nation. The only obligation for enabling a member to move such a motion is that the President/Governor or the Speaker, must give an earliest opportunity to do so, either by summoning the House if not in session, in the former case or by the Speaker, in the latter case.

Another disquieting trend which I have noticed is that there is an increasing tendency, especially on the ruling party's part, to shorten the duration of the session. It is my experience that matters of public importance generally and grievances of the people in particular are quickly dealt with when the session is on. The recent practice of setting up different committees for consideration of the budget proposals after presentation of the budget, is also intended it seems, to shorten the duration of the Session. Whatever it may be, the session's period get reduced in fact, which is not healthy. Besides the ruling party has the right to present a budget according to its own perceptions regarding matters concerning the Nation or the State and the 'opposition' has no right to suggest and bring about changes of any importance in this manner. Otherwise the whole concept of parliamentary Govt. is defeated viz. the ruling party deciding matters according to its lights and the opposition attacking them from their point of view and bidding for power on that basis, in the ensuring general elections.

I must also make a brief reference to the lectures which I delivered at the Lasky Institute in Ahmedabad and under the auspices of Sir C. P. Ramaswami Aiyer Foundation, in Madras. The subject in the former was the press and the parliamentary privileges and in the latter, the parliamentary privileges — its theory and practice. Both were well-received and have been duly printed and published. It was a great honour to me, to be in the company of distinguished public men, who had preceded me. Purushottam Mavlankar himself, former M.P., my friend and son of G. V. Mavlankar, the first Speaker of Lok Sabha had invited me for the lecture in the Lasky Institute and the foundation authorities which included the son of Sri C. P. in Madras.

Side by side with the Speakers' Conference there used to be a Conference of the Secretaries to the Parliament and the State Legislatures, which had its own agenda, for discussion and decisions. It used to be presided over by the Secretary of Lok Sabha. Kaul, the Secretary of Lok Sabha, was a dynamic person, with considerable knowledge and experience of parliamentary practice and procedure. He was greatly helped by the redoubtable Speaker of Lok Sabha, Dada Saheb Mavlankar. They together formed a formidable force to carry the country forward, in the new parliamentary field.

The questions discussed mostly pertained to the administrative field, particularly the burning question of the independence of the Legislature-Secretariats in the States and emoluments of the State-Secretaries. This had no direct impact on the State Governments, which still controlled the purse in this regard but certainly it did help in the matter. The State Legislature-secretariats were in different stages of development. In Bombay, we had our Legislative Council, before Independence and it was served by a small department headed by a Dy. Secretary of the State Govt. drawn from the I.C.S. cadre. We, therefore, had a greater difficulty to change this position. However, with persistent effort and struggle over a period of time, this was achieved. There was also the question of staff sufficient to manage the load of work during the session period. This was also achieved in due course.

The conference of the Secretaries had appointed a small committee of 5/6 Secretaries from the States — I was one of them, and this also used to meet at various places like Chandigarh, Ooty, etc. and debate and discuss matters of common interest — parliamentary and administrative.

During the period of the Conference of the Presiding Officers, there used to be programmes of sight-seeing. We had thus an opportunity of not only meeting socially and building a fraternity — of our own — but also of knowing the various states and their people, their culture and heritage — so varied and interesting in a vast country like India. We thus saw places starting from Elephanta caves, Ajanta, Ellora in Maharashtra, Khajuraho in M.P., Shillong, Cherapunji in Assam, Darjeeling and the tiger-hill to watch the reflection of the sun on Mount Everest, very early in the morning, in West Bengal, Dwarka, Bhet-Dwarka of Shree Krishna and Gir forest in Gujarat, Nagarjuna Sagar in Andhra Pradesh, Vrindavan gardens, Palaces in Mysore, Shravan Belgola, Jewel-box temples in Belur and Halebeedu in Karnataka, Mahabalipuram, Congivarum in Tamil Nadu and Kanyakumari and its confluence of the three oceans, the faintly visible Sri Lanka in the distance from the southern tip, and the Vivekanand Rock Temples in Kerala — so, varied, rich and interesting and last but not the least Kashmir —

Gulmarg, Khilan marg, Sonmarg and its forests. Being longest in service as the State Secretary, I was able to see all these places of interest and importance.

Before concluding, I would like to refer two more matters, which I consider to be of importance, in strengthening parliamentary democracy. One is the establishment of 'An Institute of Parliamentary Procedure and Practice and Constitutional Studies' to train our legislators to do their jobs efficiently, and the other is the formation of an Indian Parliamentary Service to serve properly the parliament and the State Legislatures. I tried for both these things in my time. The former had, after a number of earlier attempts, come into being during C.M. Antulay's time and I was even appointed its first director. But unfortunately Antulay had to resign shortly thereafter and Nilangekar Patil became the C.M. and he expressed misgivings about the very utility of such an Institute; I thought it was no use continuing in the post where I could do precious little, with the new C.M. holding views on it, as he did. I had even countered him by saying if the C.M. thought that there should be no library because a very small number of persons make use of it. So, I promptly resigned and the matter ended there. However, the need of such an institute is all the greater. I hope and wish, the authorities will take note of this and start taking steps to start the institution.

As regards the other thing i.e. formation of 'Indian Parliamentary Service' like I.A.S. several attempts were made in the past towards that end; but they all failed, not because it was not proper or feasible, but because of the shortsighted, monopolistic and self-interested attitude of the then Lok Sabha Secretariat.

On our persistent demands on this question, they used to set up a committee to consider the matter and at the crucial time back out, on the ground that there was no consensus in the matter and that we should wait for such a consensus. I firmly believe that such a service is absolutely necessary, and the sooner it is started, the better for all concerned, in the interest of parliamentary democracy. Then, there will be an expert independent service as in the House of Commons in England, to serve the Parliament/State Legislatures without fear or favour. I hope that this also will be taken due note of, by the authorities concerned.

Chapter IX

DEPARTMENT OF LEGISLATIVE AFFAIRS

After my final retirement as Secretary to the Legislature in 1972 April, there was an interregnum of about a year, before I was drafted again in Govt. as the Secretary to the Department of Legislative Affairs in 1973. I had put in 26 years of service, including the years of extension, which were in continuation of my service — not being re-employment. I was short of 4 years to earn full pension, on the basis of required 30 years of service. I was entitled to this weightage of service on the general principle governing weightage. In due course the necessary orders were passed giving me the weightage. I then saw the Accountant-General, Bombay, requesting him to revise my pension — my full pension — on that basis. The Accountant-General of the time was exceedingly nice to me, treated me with great respect, and even offered me tea. He called the officer in charge and instructed him to issue the necessary orders and assured me that this will be done in about 8/10 days.

The A.G. was as good as his word and I got the necessary orders in Nagpur where I had gone as Secretary to the Department of Legislative Affairs, for the winter-session of the Legislature. The Asstt. Pay and Accounts Officer of the time was equally nice and he arranged to pay the whole amount due to me at one go. Such things are rare in Govt. service, especially, after one retires.

The starting of the Department of Legislative Affairs, on the pattern of Ministry of Parliamentary Affairs in Delhi, has its own interesting story. Tidke, the Minister for Legislative Affairs, was keen to have it. The bureaucracy however was opposed to it and raised objections against it, without any valid reasons. The Department was intended to serve the Govt. for advising it on parliamentary matters — a sort of internal Audit — on the one hand and act as a liaison between the Govt. and the Legislature on the other. The Department however came into being after meeting the objections raised by them. They also raised an objection, quite untenable, regarding my appointment as its Secretary, on the grounds that a Secretary to Govt. must be from the I.A.S. cadre. So a way was found to describe my designation as Secretary to the Minister of Legislative Affairs. I agreed to it, saying that it could be set right on assuming charge of the office. During all these discussions between the Minister Tidke (Legislative Affairs) and Madhukarrao Choudhary (Finance) and the concerned Secretaries of G.A.D. and F.D. my advice was sought from my residence on the phone and it was also given on the phone sometimes, and sometimes by a special note on the subject for the Minister's use. Then there was the difficulty of getting the necessary staff to run the Department. Although everything was clear on the file for the creation of the Department, F.D. would not sanction the staff and the file remained pending in the Department (F.D.) for quite long when Antulay, Minister for Law, came to my rescue and clinched the matter. I was asked to be present in his chamber with the relevant file on a certain evening. He brought the Ministers concerned to his chamber after the cabinet meeting and obtained their signatures to it. After I assumed charge, I was able to get my designation also changed as 'Secretary to the Department of Legislative Affairs' and also the required staff, without much difficulty. I started the Department in right earnest and settled its working. I have put down detailed instructions (which have been printed) for its working in future. The Department has been functioning well.

After retirement, as Secretary to the Legislature, I felt greatly relieved and I had no feelings of regret which many people experience after the hectic period of service. I had done enough work to my satisfaction, which had also received general acceptance. During this period of interregnum, there was not much to do to speak of. Late Vishram Bedekar, the well-known literateur and his equally well-known wife Maltibai (who is still happily with us in Pune) were my neighbours. We were family friends. They were not good mixers, socially speaking, especially Vishram Bedekar, in our building at least — 'Dinath Court'. But we were good friends and had close relations. He had made me an offer for going to U.S.A. with him for a month where his only son Shrikant was settled, but I could not avail myself of it, to my eternal regret, due to various reasons. The air-fare to U.S.A. both to and fro, was only Rs.4,000/- then. To this day I have not been able to visit U.S.A., though in addition, I had an invitation in that connection from the American Govt. which for some technical reasons did not materialize. Even now, I am not sure, due to age, whether I would be able to visit that dream-country, though several members of my own family are settled there.

How my American visit failed has its own story and a moral. I had received an invitation to visit U.S.A. and go all over the continent under their 'Leadership Programme'. I told our Speaker Silam about it, so also our Chairman Page. Both of them wholeheartedly supported my visit. The C. M. Yeshwantrao also approved of it. Personally, I had thought of studying their parliamentary system and specially their powerful committees, apart from observing their Govt's, governance in general.

Our Nagpur Session was less than 2 months away—I wanted about two and half months for the visit. Silam desired that I should be back in time for the winter-session in Nagpur. So I thought of postponing the visit till after the Session. I contacted the American Consulate and sought their advice. They told me that the invitation was open for the whole year and I could safely plan my visit, anytime during the year. I therefore decided to postpone the visit. I then committed my life's blunder of writing officially to Govt. about the visit. The State Govt — i.e. G.A.D. (General Administration Department) informed me that there were instructions from Govt. of India that no govt. officer should accept an invitation directly to go abroad, unless it was routed through the External Affairs Ministry and was approved by them. Since our State Govt. i.e. C.M. had already approved of my visit, they sent the proposal with their recommendation, for the sanction of Govt. of India.

The Govt. of India however advised me to decline the invitation. Speaker Silam pleaded with M. J. Desai, the then Secretary-General of External Affairs

Ministry in that regard. He did not agree and the visit failed. It was gross injustice to me. Firstly, that circular had not been endorsed to me, though I headed an independent Department. Secondly, the circular was meant to curb top officers of Govt. capable of conferring some benefit in exchange of the wangled visit of the inviting country. I was in no position to do any such thing, since my secretariat, which I headed was not basically an administrative Department. It is pertinent to observe in this connection that, M. J. Desai, who professed to be so meticulous about such things, undertook a world tour, on the eve of his retirement, on the pretext of inspecting the embassies abroad. I remember that the *'Times of India'* carried an editorial castigating him strongly for this visit. However, my visit did not take place.

I will refer to a few things, during my tenure as the Secretary to the Department of Legislative affairs. The address of the Governor to both Houses of the Legislature is a Cabinet-document, detailing the broad programmes and policies of the Government. It is in no sense an expression of the governor's views on the administration. He, as the Head of the State, is only the mouthpiece of the government. It is based on the concept of the Queen's address to the two Houses of Parliament in England.

The President's address to the Houses of Parliament in India also is on the same pattern and governed by the same considerations. I was in-charge of preparing the address of the Governor. I used to issue a circular to all the departments of the Government, giving guidelines for supplying me the necessary material for inclusion in the address within a particular time. I used to sift that information and retain only that much, which conformed to the guidelines. I had to cut out a great deal of such information, much to the annoyance of the departments. But this had to be done if one had to remain true to the Constitution. After this stage, the prepared address that emerged, used to go before the Cabinet Sub-Committee, for scrutiny and then before the whole Cabinet, after it was whetted by the Sub-Committee, for its final approval. This was a very ticklish matter, requiring chasing the departments for the required material within the stipulated time. Sometimes I had to be harsh with the departments for this purpose.

Then I had to see that the departments do not issue ordinances without compelling reasons to do so. An ordinance is the law made by Government, in its executive capacity, an extraordinary power granted to the Government, under the Constitution, to meet the compelling circumstances. It can be done only when the Houses of the Legislature are in recess i.e. not in session and there is an urgent need to make the Law, before the Legislature could meet and enact the Law. The departments are required to place the copies of the ordinances thus issued before both the Houses of the Legislature, on the first day of the session. It was my duty to see that the ordinances were properly issued and also placed before the two Houses, on the first day, giving reasons as to why it became necessary to issue the ordinances. This care had to be taken to avoid strictures in the House. I had to act as a sort of a watchdog in this connection.

Then, I had to examine the assurances given by the ministers in the House. I had to see whether the ministerial declaration in the House, amounted to an assurance according to set formulae and further such assurances were fulfilled within reasonable time. This precaution had to be taken before the matter was placed before the Committee on Government-assurances for their scrutiny, to avoid adverse comments from them. If these things are properly done and I had to see they are so done, the work of the Government in the Legislature becomes smooth and without blemish. Besides, I had to discuss and settle with the Legislature-Secretary, points of difference if any, between the two organizations, sometimes with the ministers concerned from the government and the two presiding officers of the Legislature, being also present. I had also to attend B.A.C. (Business Advisory Committee) to settle the government business in the Legislature.

There was one ticklish matter raised in the Assembly in the Nagpur Winter Session. Late L. G. Rajwade, the Chief Secretary had occupied one of the rooms in the inspection bungalow in Pune and kept it locked for his use, after he had retired. The matter was raised in the House. D. D. Sathe, the Chief Secretary at the time asked me to sort out the matter. I advised Sathe that the only way to settle the matter was for Rajwade to say "sorry" and close the matter. It was a bitter pill for them but they had to swallow it.

During the whole period of my tenure of the secretaryship, the work ran smoothly and I finally retired after my term in 1978 with full satisfaction. During that time Shankarrao Chavan was the Chief Minister, D. D. Sathe the Chief Secretary and B. G. Deshmukh, who finally retired as the Cabinet Secretary of Government of India, as the private Secretary to the Chief Minister.

After relinquishing charge of this office I worked for some time, privately with late Rajaram Bapu Patil, a former minister of Government to assist him in Parliamentary matters. I also worked as an advisor on Parliamentary matters to the Janata Party, which had been returned to the Assembly in a large number when Sharad Pawar broke away from the Congress and allied with the Janata Party with his followers numbering about 50 forming Progressive Democratic Front. The coalition Government headed by Vasantdada Patil was reduced to a minority. I wrote letters in that connection to the Governor, and the Speaker of the Assembly, bringing this position to their notice and requesting necessary action in the matter. Shortly thereafter, Vasantdada Patil, Chief Minister resigned and Pawar was installed as Chief Minister. I continued to work with P.D.F. till Pawar's government was dismissed and the Assembly dissolved by Indira Gandhi, Prime Minister immediately after the close of the Nagpur Session, in 1980 after about a year's working.

Chapter X

LIFE IN RETIREMENT AND WORK

I settled down at my Worli residence after ceasing my connection with Government or any party in a private capacity. This must have been around 1980. I felt free and relieved and had no regrets for doing so. I had not thought much about my future plans. I used to go for morning walks on the Worli sea-face which was close and play tennis at Bombay Gymkhana in the evenings and engage myself in doing some odd things. This went on like this for some time. I had no definite plans, regarding my life in retirement. Friends suggested that I should do some social service but I had no inclination for that.

However one fine morning, Jangoo Gagrat — a well-known solicitor persuaded — prevailed on me to undertake the work of improvement of the Worli-Sea-face — one of the best sea-fronts — which was in a bad shape. He volunteered to help me in all possible ways. Soon I got myself involved in that work. We formed an informal committee to draw up plans for the improvement. Our strategy was to divide the work into convenient parts — small works and find a donor and also a person who will actually carry out the work and monitor the work till its completion, without being obliged to handle the money ourselves. There were plans to plant trees, with tree-guards along the sea front, put benches at convenient distances for people to relax, build urinals and sanitary blocks, for a large number of people, who were otherwise using the sea-side, for their morning ablutions.

One fine morning, Goel a retired Chairman of the State Bank of India, gave me a cheque for Rs. 5 lakhs, to be used for the improvement work, from the Tata Electric Companies of which he was one of the directors. We thought of using the amount for building a sufficiently large sanitary complex at the northern end of the sea-face, for use of such persons.

'Sulabha International' was engaged in the work of constructing and maintaining such blocks in a clean and hygienic manner. We contacted them and they agreed to do the job. The Bombay Municipal Corporation readily gave its permission to build the complex, on the sea-face.

The whole thing started in right earnest and it was soon completed and put into use, by charging a small fee for use of the latrines and no charge at all for use of the urinals. There was a small function arranged by us for throwing it open for public use. We had, no doubt, a few difficulties to face — even court proceedings in executing this project. Tinaikar, the then Municipal Commissioner, helped us out whenever we were in difficulties. A court case against us — the original and in appeal, was handled by Gagrat & Co., at no cost. Now I understand that they have created a sort of mini-forest surrounding the complex for people to relax and enjoy. Navroj Wadia, my friend and a neighbour in Dinath Court, produced an excellent plan for the complex, which, I believe was copied and built-upon for another similar complex at the Southern end of the sea-face, by the Municipal Corporation.

As for the cement concrete benches, the Marwadi residents in the neighbourhood, came to help us in big way. They formed their own group which paid for the large number of benches to be put on the sea-front. Navroj Wadia, the Architect — friend of mine, who was helping us a great deal in this connection, took keen interest in selecting the benches of the correct size, shape, form and colour, from an aesthetic point of view and also fixing the firm for supplying them and putting them in a manner suggested by him at quite reasonable rates. This was done quickly because there were a large number of people wanting to donate benches in memory of their kith and kin. In the course of time trees were also planted with protection guards. We also succeeded in removing hutments from the nearby area.

Our object was to improve the sea-front and its immediate surroundings. We stopped pony-riding on the sea-front which was a big nuisance and took care to see that the whole area was kept clean, tidy and safe. The work is going on; many industries like Hindustan Lever, Asian Paints, Eastern Shipping etc. have extended to us their helping hand. J. K. Kapoor, a well-known hotelier, Padwal, a senior executive in a big company, Jacob, a printer, and Bansilal Modi also a senior executive in a company and others are carrying on the work further. I still continue to be their nominal chairman even after I left Bombay.

Again, I soon got involved at the request of late Laljibhai Mehrotra, Consul-General of Japan (Retd.) in the work of senior citizens. For me, the idea was completely new and I did not think that any good would come out of it. I was nominally there as the Secretary of the Association for senior citizens. I must confess that I did no work in that connection, the whole burden being borne by Laljibhai. Khandpur, a retired chairman of the Film Censor Board, was also a member. In fact, at one time, we both thought of withdrawing from that body.

But, then Laljibhai died suddenly in the train, when he was travelling to Ahmedabad. Vinaybhai Mehrotra, his son was completely at sea and did not know how to go about this work. He had just retired from service and come to stay at Worli, and was therefore quite ignorant of this project. But he was a determined man and was anxious to continue and carry forward this and other good works, started by his distinguished father. At that point of time, we, myself and Khandpur decided to remain fully involved in the work. I was its Chairman for 4/5 years, after my distinguished predecessors like, Laljibhai, the founder-President, Ganatra, the former mayor of Bombay and late B. K. Patil, I.C.S. Retd. I continued to be the Chairman and did some useful work, with the active help and cooperation of Vinaybhai, Khandpur, Shivraj Bahadur and others, till I retired after my term, and on my leaving Bombay for good to settle in Pune.

I get regular reports about their on-going activities and they are doing an excellent job, now under the able stewardship of the President, Shivraj Bahadur. Khandpur has been its senior Vice-President for the last several years. He is very active and takes full part in the activities of the Association. For some unaccountable reasons, he has declined to be its Chairman. K. C. Malhotra has been doing an excellent job as the General Secretary. Both he and Khandpur have been my close friends. They have also, very kindly, made me a patron of this Association, for whatever little work I may have done. But I have earned their friendship and love for me, which they have indicated to me in several ways. Quite recently they did me great honour, on my completion of 89 years of age, by presenting me with an excellent shawl and a souvenir — emblem of the Association through the Secretary Paigankar.

I have been a member of the Karnatak Progressive Education Society, its new Avatar from its earlier sectarian name. This was so changed because of its earlier caste-denomination, which was no longer in vogue. It has completed 50 years of very useful service of helping poor promising students, who desired to prosecute higher studies like medical, engineering, etc. The scheme provided an interest-free loan to the students to be paid every year, provided he maintained his progress satisfactorily. It did not help the student fully but helped in a substantial way. He was to return the loan in easy instalments after he started earning.

Thus, nearly more than 1000 students have been helped so far and most of them are doing very well, and have become useful and worthy citizens of India. Now several such schemes, including those of the banks are in operation, helping poor students in a big way. But ours was a pioneering effort and it has paid off very well. We celebrated its golden jubilee recently and it was graced by the presence of Mrs. Justice Sujata Manohar, a Judge of the Bombay High Court. Ram Joshi, the former Vice Chancellor of the Bombay University, who himself was a recipient of such assistance and M. S. Gore, the former Director of Tata

Institute of Social Sciences and also the Vice-Chancellor of Bombay University, who also addressed the gathering.

I have been its President for the last many years. But the real solid work is being done by Hunshikatti, Bhujang and Masur, among others. My predecessors, have been great names — viz. Mr. Justice N. S. Lokur, R. A. Jahagirdar and others. This was started through the farsightedness of the friends like Dr. Bhagirthrao Deshpande and K. A. Kabbur, a colour-magnate. We are trying to diversify its activities by trying to help students wishing to go abroad for further studies. We have already started helping Sanskrit Pathshalas and some hostels for the students. It has been excellent activity for which we should all be proud.

I have also been associated with the Poorna Prajna Education Centre of Dahisar founded by one of the pontiffs of Udipi — Swamiji of Admar Math Shri Vibhudeshwar Swami. It caters to the pupils in preprimary, primary and secondary schools — numbering about 4000. I have been the Chairman of its governing Council for the past many years. Since coming over to Pune, I have ceased to be active in its work. Vibhudeshwar Swamiji of Admar Math, Udipi, has been a great builder of such institutions, spread all over India, including Delhi, Bangalore, and a string of educational institutions in Udipi itself, covering several disciplines. Swamiji is trying to build a big research institute for our talented students. It is a very ambitious project costing several hundred crores of rupees. He has created a network in U.S.A. for collecting funds in a big way.

Meanwhile, he has started helping a few students, who have been studying in the prestigious science institute of Bangalore. Recently the centre completed 25 years of useful service and celebrated its Silver Jubilee. I feel greatly honoured by my association with an organization like this. The stamp of Swamiji's great personality pervades in all the institutions started by him.

I have also been connected with the religious-cum-educational activities in the shape of 'Satya-Dhyan Vidyapeeth' of Mulund. It was founded by another great man, the late Gopalacharya Mahuli who dedicated himself fully for the growth and progress of this Institution. It trains young boys between the ages of 8-10 years, in all our Shastric literature, especially of Shri Madhwacharya's School of Philosophy 'Dwaitism'.

They are also given conventional education, so that they can if they so desire, follow the general way of life like many others. They have produced during the course of the last many years, brilliant scholars like Jayateerth Malagi, Ph.D., Ramacharya Nagarhalli, among others.

Already, several scholars have left after completion of their course of training for about 12 years in the Gurukul fashion, and have established themselves in places like Belgaum, Bijapur, Ainapur, etc. The trainees live there absolutely free of cost and are cared for in every way, for their progress and betterment. The Vidyapeeth is fortunate in having Vidyasinhacharya, son of Gopalacharya, the founder, as its Kulapati, who is equally well-versed and is carrying this great burden on his young shoulders. He is also being helped by his uncle Ashwathamacharya, and brother-in-law, Krishnacharya, who are erudite scholars and dedicated to the cause.

It is difficult to lead a life of austerity, service, and sacrifice, in the midst of temptations of looking on the other side of the hedge, especially for a person so young and full of promise. But shunning all temptations, he is carrying the cross, to the great satisfaction of every one. There are both religious, cultural and educational activities spread over, throughout the year. Today there are about 120 boys receiving this training. The Institution is sustained mainly by donations and offerings of the public, who receive its benefits.

D. K. Rao, one of the senior Executives of the Tatas, is the President of the Vidyapeeth. Both he and his wife Ratnamma are fully dedicated to the cause. They are deeply religious and lead an orthodox life as enjoined by Vaishnava Dharma. D. K. is a strict disciplinarian and the Institution is safe in his hands. They are naturally our family friends. I would strongly advise study of Sanskrit at least, in this Institution. Gopalacharya was a great man of knowledge and erudition fully dedicated to the cause, chosen as his life's mission. I have seen this Institution grow from its small beginning to the gigantic stature to which it has grown. Unfortunately, it has received very little publicity, but its value in terms of service it is rendering to the society is none the less very great. I have been very fortunate in associating myself with this great centre, from its very early days, not in any official capacity, but as one interested in its great work, particularly in its manifold functions and activities.

In Worli, we have another great Institution known as the King George V Memorial. It comprises two institutions, (1) Infirmary (2) Home for the destitute (converted into beggars' home). The Infirmary has a capacity to keep 100 inmates, who are patients requiring long term treatment, after being discharged from the hospital. The Home for the destitute was originally so, but later on converted into a regular beggars' home, under Government orders, Government entering into an agreement with the home for its maintenance, on the basis of rates specified for various items. The relationship of the home with the Government was entirely governed by this agreement and the audit also based its examination and comments, relying on this agreement.

The home has a capacity to keep about 300 inmates, male and female and they are all accommodated including the inmates of the Infirmary, in a number of barracks constructed for the purpose. A bright chap from the audit, raised an objection that the grant to be paid by Govt. as per agreement, was not admissible on the ground that the management had been also in receipt of the Municipal grant. This objection was upheld even by the higher authorities of Govt. and consequently the grant which used to be paid all along, was withheld.

No argument would convince the Govt. about the wrong they were commiting. The whole fallacy of the matter consisted in the assumption that the beggars' home was a grant-in-aid institution, the amount of the grant being varied according to its needs, taking into account its resources from other sources, if any. This assumption vas totally wrong, because the beggars' home based its claim on the basis of the special agreement with Govt. which was being acted upon all along by Govt. the audit including. However, Govt. struck to its view and the grant was stopped. I have no doubt if we had gone to court, we would have won hands down.

In these circumstances, we received an attractive offer from Ambani, a business magnate, proposing that they would build a speciality hospital at a cost of about 60 crores of rupees, using some portion of the vacant land, in the possession of the memorial. We drew up an MOU (Memorandum of Understanding) with them and after a number of joint meetings with them, finalized the MOU. It was to be a charitable institution, keeping certain beds free including surgery beds, the remaining beds being charged at rates sufficient to cover the loss on account of free beds. It was, in no way, to be used for any commercial purpose. The news regarding this got abroad, and a section of the press hostile to Ambanis attacked writing adversely on the scheme saying that Ambanis were exploiting the Memorial for their own benefit. This was quite wrong. The Govt. even otherwise grants lands for charitable causes. One did not understand, what mattered if Ambanis came forward to fulfil some charitable purpose. One must also bear in mind that Dhirubhai Ambani, the principal person, had suffered a paralytic stroke and was also perhaps a heart-patient. It was natural for him to turn his attention to some charitable cause. The Memorial has about 13 acres of prime-land, located in the center of the city and Ambanis were going to use only about 3/4 acres of it. Besides, they had also agreed to build a sufficiently large building to accommodate both the inmates of the Infirmary and also those of the beggars' home i.e. altogether about 400 inmates. In addition they had agreed to set apart one and half crores of rupees, earning enough interest to maintain the beggars' home, whose grant was stopped by Govt.

With the adverse publicity in the press, some of our members, including specially Govt. Secretaries and the Municipal Commissioner, developed cold feet and the whole scheme was shelved. This was the tragic end of an excellent proposal and Bombay lost a prestigious hospital in a central place. To this day, I regret the whole thing. Dr. Manelikar, Head of the Orthopedic Department of K.E.M. Hospital, had taken great pains in the matter to prepare notes and carefully build up the whole case. Shortly after this, I also ceased to be a member of Managing Committee.

Prof. Gokak, as he was usually known, had been awarded the most prestigious award of ज्ञानपीठ for literature. I had not come into contact with him, though I used to read about him and his activities. I, as the President of the Karnataka Progressive Education Society, along with the Chairman Hunshikatti, Secretary Masur and Dr. Kanbur called on him at his residence to felicitate him for the award. He and his wife received us and we had a hearty talk for nearly two hours, Gokak narrating his experiences and other things.

He had gone to the Oxford University for M.A. in English. He had completed the course and appeared for the written examination. The viva-voce was to take place a little later. Gokak decided to utilize this free time and went to Edinburgh in Scotland. He developed suddenly an acute pain in the stomach, which was no ordinary pain, but an attack of appendicitis. He was immediately taken on the operation table for an emergency operation. The operation was successful and he started recovering. He decided in his mind that the rest of the remaining life, which has been saved, would be devoted to the service of God. He then wrote to the university authorities about his viva-voce examination saying that he had to miss it, because of his sudden illness and operation. He desired to know what next.

The authorities informed him that they had examined his written-papers and have already declared him to have passed in Ist class and that there was no need for him to appear for viva-voce any longer.

A thought crossed my mind as to what would have happened in India, in a similar situation. I am sure that he would have lost the year and would have been required to appear for the examination next year. I have narrated this as he (Gokak) himself related to us. Both were great, the University of Oxford as also Prof. Gokak. We returned after making small presents to both of them as a token of our admiration and affection; a few photographs have been taken on the occasion. I cherish today the happy memory of the memorable visit. Prof. Gokak died some time ago.

"Dinath Court", the name of the building where I lived, is an old building, very well-built, but not maintained properly by timely repairs, mainly for want of funds. We, tenants, paid very little rent, the rent that was in vogue in 1945 or so. Prices, had during the years, skyrocketed, while rents of old buildings had remained pegged at a very low level. The building has about 12 huge flats, 9 four bed-roomed and 3, three bed-roomed. Rooms and the halls were spacious, say, even luxurious. Tenants, were all old tenants paying rent at the 1945 level, which was ridiculously low. The property 'Dinath' was owned by a Muslim trust, which ran a hospital at Surat and also owned other properties in Bombay and Surat. I went there to live in a 3 bed-roomed flat in 1970 which was de-requisitioned by Govt. on the condition that the landlord accepted me as a direct tenant, with full benefits of the rent Act. Mohammed Dinath, the Managing Trustee, was a nice man, who managed the property as best as he could, within the limited income from the rents.

I was approached by A. K. Mohamed's son, (who had in the meanwhile become the Managing Trustee) to do something about the repairs to the building. We formed a sort of informal Maintenance Committee, of which I became the Chairman. We set about the work, carried out the necessary repairs, and also built an underground tank for adequate supply of water, which had become necessary, owing to a number of new constructions in the area. The cost of Rs. 6 lakhs or so was readily contributed by us tenants, including the landlord. The work was executed at very reasonable rates because of the good offices of Chari, ex-Income Tax Commissioner, who was also living there. All the tenants were nice people and we had no difficulty in carrying out the work. Mrs. Nasrulla, a former Sheriff of Bombay, was one of the tenants and we held our periodical meetings in her flat. Altogether I have happy memories of my stay in the Dinath Court, all the tenants forming one big family. There were Hindus, Muslims, Parsees and Christians and we all lived happily. Contractor was our treasurer, who kept regular accounts and got them audited regularly. Navroj Wadia, an architect, was advising us on the repairs and construction part. He is very resourceful and does his work painstakingly. He was particularly attached to our family. Whenever he comes to Pune, we always meet and lunch together in a hotel. He is very generous and hospitable. I wish, I had continued to stay there, instead of moving to Pune, which was a big mistake, on my part.

Every Thursday evening, my wife and I used to go to Matunga — 'Vani-Vihar Vidyalaya' for devotional songs, sung by women who attended regularly. N. R. Rao used to come all the way from his Malabar Hill residence, to pick up us and leave us at our door, after the bhajans. He did not fail to do so even once. Late Gopalacharya used to remain present and would explain the meaning and implications of one of these songs sung. My wife Padmavati liked such programmes more than functions at the club — Bombay Gymkhana. She was genuinely interested in such activities and I was drawn to it, because of her interest in the matter. She also sang one or two songs on the occasion. Her bent of mind was spiritual and she was easily attracted to such activities. We had formed a good fraternity. D. K. Rao, the President of the Vidyapeeth, and Ratnamma, his wife took great interest in the progress and development of this institution—they were fully dedicated to this cause. D. K. Rao and his wife Ratnamma, N. R. Rao and his wife Malati, Swamirao and his family members, and we, had become close family friends and happily still continue to be so. I am missing all this, in Pune.

Padmavati, my wife, was a remarkable woman by all accounts. She was a person of rare courage and confidence and was a great support to me in all what I did. She helped me freely with her gold ornaments, when we needed money, for the support of the family and other things. She was very talented and had quick grasp of things. She had a great knack of making friends and she was extremely popular with them. She had hardly studied upto 4th Std. English, but she acted with full confidence in any company of men and women, who were highly educated, holding big positions in the society. She was equally free and popular with menials like maid servants, sweepers etc.

She was closely connected with the women's organization 'Mahila Vikas Mandal', Colaba, a highbrow society — of highly educated women drawn from the affluent and powerful families of high Govt. officials, right from its inception, and worked for many years either as its treasurer or Vice President. She was even offered the Presidentship of this body — but she declined it. It is very rare for such things to happen. She worked closely for many years with Sushilatai Joshi (wife of late D.S. Joshi, I.C.S., who was the Cabinet Secretary of Govt. of India) in connection with a rescue home for women in Bombay. She was a member of State Women's Welfare Board, working with late Kusumtai Wankhede (Finance Minister's wife) who was its chairperson. She did her work quietly and unostentatiously. I was amazed to see a large number of persons, visiting me to pay condolences, on her demise. There were also very touching letters from many others in that connection.

She spoke Kannada, Marathi and Hindi, quite fluently and even English fairly well. Among her friends may be mentioned, Sharada Mukherjee, the former Governor of Gujarat and Andhra Pradesh, Nirmala Raje Bhonsale, ex-Minister of Govt. of Bombay/ Maharashtra, Kanchanmala-Raje Bhosale, Ranisaheb of Nagpur, Malatibai Bedekar, an illustrious writer and author of many books in Marathi, Narmadabai Samarth, a well-known educationist, Lokurs, Deshmukhs and late Kedars and Malustes — who are still our family friends. She had absolutely no stage fright and could participate with ease, in Radio programmes, dramas (Marathi and Kannada) and public functions.

She always took great care of her health, which she maintained fairly well. She was very practical and never hesitated or delayed in obtaining the necessary medical treatment whenever she felt the slightest need for it. She was one of the very few persons, who got herself checked up, for cancer, in the cancer society, every year. This may be because both her parents died prematurely of cancer. She had to undergo a few surgical operations. Eminent doctors like Shirodkar, Ginde, Talwalkar and Purandare had become our family friends. Quite a few of our close relatives came to Bombay for medical treatment, among whom may be mentioned late Vijayarao Chebbi (my sister's son-in-law) and my brother's wife Akkutai. She literally saved Vijayarao (who was operated for brain tumur, by Ginde) who, a few days after the operation, developed high fever in the Bombay hospital. My wife was alone in the room (it was lunch time) with the patient. She just took off the needle (for glucose treatment) and rushed to the doctor in charge for looking into the case. The doctor profusely thanked her for what she had done as the high fever was the result of some impurity in the glucose. By quick and expert treatment, the fever was brought down. So the life was saved.

In the other case, Dr. Shirodkar made her wear an apron and watch the operation, which she did. He even discharged the patient, when the wound had not been fully healed saying that Mrs. Belavadi would know how to dress the wound which she did it quite successfully. When Akkutai had gone there for delivery, later on, my wife who was in attendance, noticed some defect in the infant which Dr. Shirodkar corrected by a small operation. She had that rare uncanny sense. Although, I was entitled to free medical treatment in a Govt. hospital, we never went there and my wife always went to a private hospital of her friends, where she was sure of proper care and treatment. It was also free. When I was operated for prostate by Dr. Ajit Phadke, my wife was with me all the time, taking care of me, the household matters being left to be attended to, by our helper Rajaram Madhyasta. Her singleminded devotion was a great support and solace to me and I recovered and made rapid progress towards normal health.

When she married me and came to our house, she became one with our family in every sense, admired and loved by all. This is also very rare. When she died suddenly in June 1992, one can imagine my plight. I did not know what to do. I was alone with her in the flat. However my friends rendered me great help in every way and I was not required to do anything in the matter. This was my great fortune that so much goodwill was there for us.

During my spare time I read great many books, mostly in English, French and Sanskrit, a few in Marathi and Kannada. I used to borrow books from Nirmala Raje Bhonsale, who had an excellent collection of books, in English and French. Books are an excellent company especially for lonely souls and they give great pleasure and entertainment apart from knowledge. I read only books of well-known authors, which are classics of a kind. Among these may be mentioned, biography of Samuel Pepse, the father of British Civil Service, Viceroys' Journal by Lord Wavel, our last Viceroy, 3rd French Republic, detailing the significant events of 2nd World-War, started by Hitler, the German dictator, including General De' Gaule's great contribution, when French Generals had just developed cold feet and left the field clear for the Germans to occupy, complete works of Goldsmith, with its excellent introduction, detailing the state of 'polite learning' meaning literature in Europe, works of Oscar Wilde, Tolstoy's great books, like Anna Karenina, War & Peace, Resurrection etc. Dostovsky's Brothers Karamazao, Crime and Punishment, George Sand, the celebrated woman author under a man's name, the books of Victor Hugo, Les Miserables and Hunchback of Notredam, whose funeral was attended by a huge unprecedented crowd of Frenchmen and women, Rodin the world famous sculptor, Shriniwas Shastri's Lectures on Ramayana etc. in English, Symphony Pastoral by Andre Gide which made him a Nobel laureate, Le rouge etnoir... by Stendhal, biography of Victor Hugo's Mother, biographies of Emili Zola, Disrali — all in French, रणांगण, एक झाड व दोन पक्षी and ब्रम्हकुमारी, by Vishram Bedekar, व्यासपर्व by Durga Bhagwat in Marathi, Kannada translation of Manohar Malgaonkar's 'Devils Wind' describing Indian mutiny in 1957 and a sort of biography of Nana Saheb Peshwa, (the last Peshwa), the biography of German doctor Albert Schweitzer, who spent all his life, caring for the health of Africans in Africa, also a Nobel Laureate and the last but not the least, the great classics in Sanskrit by Kalidasa — अभिज्ञान शाकुंतलम्, मेघदूतम्, कुमारसंभवम्, रघुवंशम्, and वाल्मिकाग्निमित्र, and some portions of वाल्मिकी रामायण. I am mentioning only a few important books, among others.

Because of the books, of which I am very fond, I did not find time hanging over my head. Earlier I had studied French, all by myself mainly on the basis of two very good books — Teach yourself French, Book I, Elementary and Book II advanced.

I have always been fascinated by Shri Triupati of Lord Venkateshwar, which I have been visiting right from late 1930s or early 1940s. I used to go there every year in the company of Pralhadrao Kadkol — my wife's cousin, Shreedharrao Kadkol, my wife's uncle and Anantrao Kulkarni, my wife's sister's husband. They were also as fascinated and devoted, as I was, or rather I should say that I got the inspiration and a kind of provocation in the matter by their zeal and determination to visit the place and have दर्शन, of the Lord of the Hills. It was a long and strenuous journey (from Belgaum) — upto Guntakal by M.S.M. Railway and further on to Reniguntha by broad-gauge Central Railway train and thereafter, short branch-line upto Tirupati East — called also Govindraj Pattan, which was at the foot of the seven hills. From there one had to climb and cross the hills, the first climb — a very difficult one — consisting of about 2200 high stone-steps upto 'Ghali (windy) Gopuram' and then a distance of about 7 miles, climbing and descending upto the Tirumalai hills, seat of the far famed temple of Lord Venkatapati. We used to reach Tirupati early morning, proceed to 'Kapil Teerth' for the ritual bath and then start climbing on foot, entrusting our small baggage to a coolie, who would carry it to our destination there.

There were no big crowds in those days and one could easily have दर्शन, of the Lord, of course, at the stated times, either for doing some kind of सेवा (service) at the prescribed rates of fees or otherwise free धर्मदर्शन. Sevas (service) started everyday from very early morning with सुप्रभातम् with songs sung sonorously by the अर्चकाज, i.e. priests, in Tamil to awaken the

Lord so to say and then open a series of doors about 3 of outer rooms until one reached the Sanctum Sanctorum where a large, over six feet tall idol in black stone, stood with शंख, चक्र, गदा and पदम् with its forehead, part of the chin and eyes covered with श्रीपाद रेणू (a kind of special paste) an idol, at once beautiful and inspiring spontaneous devotion in the devotees. There are a series of सेवा(s) like तुलसी अर्चना, one long, 1000 names the other short (108 names) — sevas consisting in offering तुलसी leaves, तोमाल सेवा offering garlands of big roses of various sizes from the top किरीट crown to the bottom, आमंत्रण सेवा (a combination of these sevas) एकांत सेवा night service for putting the Lord to sleep, everyday besides sevas on fixed days in the week, like पुनकाभिषेक ceremonial bath with waters from पापनाशिनी and आकाशगंगा (sacred places) on Fridays 'Pulangi' covering the deity with flowers, on certain days and so on. Every seva has its fixed rate of fees, for which tickets have to be purchased before-hand. We used to do some seva either तुलसी अर्चना or तोमाल सेवा and also have धर्मदर्शन whenever available, so as to have Lord's Darshan to our heart's content. We cooked our own food, spent most of the time in the temple premises and sometimes visiting पापनाशिनी तीर्थ and आकाशगंगा तीर्थ, a few miles away. We stayed there for 2/3 days, following this routine and then returned to our destinations back. This went on, year after year— I must have visited the place more than 20 times and followed this routine in the same company. Later on roads were built, a multitude of buildings sprang up dotting the entire area; then came up also a number of rest houses, hotels etc. — a sort of tourist centre — as it were. The crowds of tourists everyday, run into several thousands. Lately, I have been visiting the place off and on, though not every year, with a gap of 2/3 years. A few years ago, we (our family members and Rao and Mrs. Rao) visited the temple, all the arrangements being looked after by Rao and my brother Appa. My latest visit was in April this year (1999) in the company of my brother Appa, sister Indu Dhumale and her daughter Anjali Apte. It was a short and quick visit, but quite satisfactory.

Once I received a letter — a customary letter to the followers — from the Swamiji of Pejawar Math, Udipi, asking me to go to Shri Badrinath during his चातुर्मास stay there. I had no idea of going there, thinking that it was too difficult to do so. But my brother Appa immediately decided to go and even purchased his ticket. I casually mentioned this to N. R. Rao, on one of the Thursdays, while returning from Matunga after 'भजन' when Appa was also accompanying us. Rao at once decided to go and also prevailed upon me to join, saying he would make all the necessary arrangements for comfortable travel and accommodation and that I need have no fear of any hardship, inconvenience or discomfort. So we all decided to go in September 1992 soon after my wife's demise in June that year. A party of six persons, myself, Appa, his wife Sunanda, my sister's daughter Sushila Chebbi, Rao and his wife Malati. We travelled by Rajdhani Express to Delhi and did the remaining part of the journey by road, in special cars. We visited Rishikesh, Haridwar, and Badrinath, where we spent 3 days. On our way back, we went up to Gourikund, from where one has to go on foot, or on a pony to reach Shri Kedarnath. Only Rao and Sunanda, Appa's wife went upto Kedarnath and we stayed back at Gourikund, for a day or so. Then we all returned back to Bombay after 8/9 days. Somehow I felt, I had not had a proper Darshan of Badrinath — Shri Narayan.

I had no doubt दर्शन of Lord नारायण 2/3 times — but not to my heart's content. This was a passing feeling, but otherwise, the visit was well-planned and well-executed. The whole journey was amidst Himalayan ranges along the river अलकनंदा upto Badrinath and a diversion at रुद्रप्रयाग for Kedarnath along मंदाकिनी river, both merging in the भागिरथी and all later in the Ganges, flowing into the plains of Rishikesh. There were unforgettable and awe-inspiring scenes all along the way. Thus I was able to visit Shri Badrinath, thanks to Rao and Appa.

In the same way, we visited Udipi, a place in South India, which is famous for its ancient temple of Lord Shree Krishna, who gave भगवत् गीता to the humanity for its salvation. Legend has it that at Malpe, a sea-coast-place nearby, Madhwacharya, the great philosopher, Saint of South India happened to see a ship — in great distress because of a heavy storm in the sea and that he saved it from drowning, by just moving his outer garment, which he was wearing. The ship came safely to the coast and the captain of the ship being overjoyed, offered to give whatever the saint desired, from the rich merchandise, it was carrying. The Saint pointed to a little mound of yellow earth (गोपीचंद) lying in a corner and said that he should like to have it and nothing more. The captain was amazed at such a request but complied with it, as the Saint was very keen to have it. The mound was broken and a beautiful idol of श्रीकृष्ण emerged out of it. It is this idol which has been installed at Udipi more than 700 years ago. It is a great pilgrim centre, which is visited by hundreds of people, everyday, for श्रीकृष्ण दर्शन. Madhwacharya, the proponent of dualism in Indian

Philosophy, has established 8 मठस् i.e. Monasteries, with 8 pontiffs, who take their turns of worship of 'श्रीकृष्ण' every two years, by rotation.

The worship is being carried on in this fashion to this day. The temple is open for दर्शन all the time of the day without any restriction, unlike the position in Shri Tirupati. The centre is also known for its feeding of the pilgrims, who flock there everyday, free of cost. The Udipi pontiffs, specially those of भंडार केरी, Admar and Pejawar maths, have been doing great work — propagating Madhwa-philosophy, and in addition, doing social and educational work in a big way.

I happen to be closely associated with one of these educational Institutions by Admar Math Swamiji in Dahisar, Bombay, Poorna Pradhnya Education Centre as the Chairman of its governing council for the last many years. We visited nearby places like पाजक क्षेम where Madhwacharya was born and grew up, Malpe the sea-coast place just mentioned and Durga Hill temple. We also visited 'धर्म क्षेत्र' a religious place about 50 Kms away, where thousands of persons flock everyday and nearly 4000/5000 persons are fed everyday free. It runs several educational institutions under the expert management of Hegdes. We returned after 4 days in Udipi. We did the entire journey by road in a special vehicle along the sea-coast highway — the entire arrangements being made as usual by Rao and my brother Appa. We were a party of about 9 persons— 5 from our family and the rest from Rao's (Appa, Sunanda, Vijayrao, Sushila and myself formed our party). We are specially beholden to Admar Math— Swamiji who took great pains to make our stay comfortable. He took us to Admar village, where he runs a junior college, which caters to the pupils of the nearby villages. Pupils living in their own villages, attend the college everyday and return back to their villages after the college hours. The college is uptodate in all its equipment and it fulfills a great need of the rural people.

I would suggest a similar plan in regard to Industry. There should be feeder or main industries in some suitable central place, where workers living in their own villages — not more than 5 miles away — would come everyday for work and return to their villages back after the work, even as the farmers who go to their lands about 4/5 miles away — work there till evening and return home by nightfall. Industries in this way need not spend on any infrastructure like houses, schools, dispensaries etc. for the workers at the factory sites. Instead, they could provide these facilities in the villages themselves enriching them in the process at relatively lower cost, with Govt. also lending a helping hand in the endeavour. This is mutually advantageous both to the industry and the Govt. It will also help reduce considerably the influx of people from the villages to the cities, creating slums everywhere.

In the same way, we visited मंत्रालयम् on the bank of Tungabhadra River, in the south where the great saint 'Raghavendra Swami' is supposed to have taken a living 'समाधी' about 400 years ago. People of all castes and creeds visit the 'समाधी' everyday for 'सेवा' and it is supposed to be a wish-fulfilling place, by the grace of the great saint. It has recently grown into a big centre with so many Govt. Rest Houses and other rest houses provided by the Math and private parties. We stayed there for two days, did our 'सेवा' and returned to our destinations. (This time, there were with us Ramans — father, mother and their grownup son accompanying Rao from Bombay and we joined them at Pune in the train. My younger sister Indu (Mrs. Dhumale), Appa and his wife Sunanda and my nephew Avinash and myself formed our party from Pune. Arrangements for the journey, accommodation at the centre and facilities for 'सेवा' were as usual looked after by the two, Rao and Appa, with their usual care and efficiency and made things easy for us. We added another family of Ramans to our group.

An unexpected bonanza came my way when Appa mentioned to me sometime in August this year (1999) that Rao was planning to visit Shri Badrinath in September, again and whether I would like to join. We immediately jumped at the idea, and decided to join. Rao drew up a detailed programme which included besides Kedarnath, Gangotri also. Eventually we six, from our family (viz. Appa, Indu (Mrs. Dhumale) Sushila (Mrs. Chebbi), Papa Vasant (sister's son) and his wife Malati from Belgaum, and myself decided to join. Papa informed me at the eleventh hour (when he came to know of our projected visit) that he would like to join with his wife Malati and whether they could be accommodated even at that late hour. Rao kindly agreed to accommodate them and Rao's party also consisted of 6 persons (viz. his two nieces from Bangalore and Kakinada, three of his friends and himself). We however decided to travel by air upto Delhi and join them there. They were to travel by train from Bombay so as to reach Delhi a little earlier. We stayed at Maharashtra Sadan in Delhi, where we had made reservations earlier.

After a good night's halt and rest, we all started in a special mini-bus in the morning for Rishikesh and reached it in the afternoon. After spending the night at Dayanand Ashram which provided for all of us, good and comfortable accommodation and also meals at night, free of cost, we started for Badrinath in the same bus next day morning. We reached Badrinath a little late in the evening. We occupied our rooms, two in each. We, six of our family party decided to stay at Badrinath for 3 days, so as to have sufficient time for Shree Narayan's Darshan and for our 'सेवा'. Rao's party left for Kedarnath after a stay of one and half days. We performed 'सेवा' अभिषेक, पूजा early morning at 5.30 a.m. on two days and had good and satisfying दर्शन of Lord (नारायण) Narayan, who after अभिषेक was covered with 'गंध' (Sandalwood-paste) all over his body and then adorned with usual apparel and 'अलंकार'. It is an excellent idol in black stone, in a sitting position ('पद्मासन') with a benign smiling look. I tried to store that image in my mind so that I could recall it, in the course of पूजा (worship) every morning and prayers at night before going to bed. We also performed 'विष्णु सहस्त्रनाम' seva in the two evenings during the stay. All the arrangements after Delhi were made through Gadwal Transport Corporation — a public undertaking of U. P. Government — accommodation including, at various places. (After our 3 days' stay at Badrinath, we joined the other party at Sialsaur on the way to Kedarnath. The other party was to reach that place from Kedarnath, where they had gone a little earlier. We all then proceeded to Gangotri (गंगोत्री) the source of the river Ganges and after visiting that place we returned to Rishikesh, with a night's halt at Utter

Kashi (उत्तरकाशी) on the way. And then after a day's halt at Rishikesh, left for Delhi, which we reached in the afternoon.

We, six went to Maharashtra Sadan, had a good wash, a good lunch and some rest before we left for the airport to return to Pune, where we reached in the evening. The other party, went by train to their respective places. The whole visit lasted for nearly 10 days and we all enjoyed our cherished visit. Gadwal Corporation makes all the arrangements, and one has to carry only one's clothing. I was full of misgivings for the visit, mainly because of my advanced age and also because of a little trouble with my left foot, which made walking somewhat difficult, particularly if the distance was too long. However, with Lord Shri Narayana's grace and in the company of our family members and dear friends, to help me if needed, everything went off nicely without any trouble or difficulty.

Chapter XI
FRIENDSHIPS — I CHERISH

In the course of my life covering nearly 9 decades, I have made many friends and acquaintances, at various stages, and levels and in diverse fields. I propose to mention only a few of them, who have had some impact on my life.

At school and college, mention may be made of Haribhau Saraf, Shreedhar Garde and Shankar now Satish Kalelkar. Haribhau was my schoolmate and collegemate, right from 2nd standard English. We used to be always together and I was a constant and regular visitor to his house. His mother, who was also a mother to me, was a noble lady par excellence. She had become a widow at a very early age, and she led a pious and austere life. Haribhau grew up under her care and attention. He naturally developed a strong character without any blemish. He was a great help to me in my early life, both financially and even otherwise. It was he, who changed the course of my life and prevailed on me to go in for Law, when I had intended to study science and become an M.Sc. and follow a teaching career.

Of course, I have no regrets since everything turned out very well, all to my advantage and prosperity. We remained close friends till he died a few years ago. Because of us, our two families also had become quite close. His mother suffered a paralytic stroke and was bed-ridden. Whenever I visited them, I used to sit close near her bed and she would treat me with kindness and affection, like her own son. Haribhau did not succeed in his scholastic career, as he led an easy-going life. He left education, became a medical representative and earned enough money by sheer hard work. I lost a good and honest friend in his death, which was somewhat premature. I have not been able to keep any regular contacts with that family after his death, but the family is doing well.

Shreedhar Garde and Satish Kalelkar were at school with me in the Matriculation class — we passed the matriculation examination together. Both Garde and Kalelkar went to Baroda College, Baroda, for the first year in Arts, as Garde's elder brother had joined the Kala Bhavan Technical Institute, at Baroda and Kalelkar, because probably of the proximity of the place to Ahmedabad, where he had lived in Sabarmati Ashram of Gandhiji. Kalelkar had left the Ashram and come to Shahapur for his matriculation as his mother's sister Mrs. Shirodkar was living there. Haribhau and myself opted for the Baroda College for I.Sc. because our friends Garde and Kalelkar were already there. Because of Kalelkar, we visited Ahmedabad, saw Sabarmati Ashram and even joined the early morning prayers on the bank of Sabarmati river. Kakasaheb Kalelkar, a noted literary figure and a close associate of Gandhiji was then the vice-chancellor of the Gujarat Vidyapeeth. Both Haribhau and Garde failed in the I.Sc. examination and Kalelkar joined the Dandi March for salt satyagraha, leaving his career.

During those years, we were very close friends and enjoyed each others' company fully. Garde passed his I.Sc. the next year and joined the Grant Medical college, Bombay. I was instrumental in securing a part-time job for him in a local English school, where I had joined as a teacher, either because he needed it or just for the fun of teaching. In course of time both Kalelkar, after his graduation from the Elphinstone college and Garde after his M.B.B.S. went to England for higher studies. But, after their return from abroad both showed no interest in continuing our friendship for reasons, I am unable to comprehend, and my one-way approach to them proved fruitless. Thus, for all practical purposes our cherished friendship came to an end. Dr. Garde after his stint in the Army Service in the 2nd World War and medical practice for some years, settled down at Lonavala near Pune, during his retirement. I happened to meet him, much later, at the time of Mrudula's (my niece) marriage in Pune with Sudhir, the son of Admiral Soman. He had attended the marriage at the invitation of Admiral Soman, who was his close friend for many years. Garde died a few years ago.

Kalelkar after his return from Oxford, joined Indian Foreign Service and retired in due course. I believe that he is still living in Delhi but I have had no contact with him. I must also mention another similar case concerning one, Hebbalkar, who was my neighbour in Tukaram Ashram, Pune, when I was studying in S. P. College. In spite of my rushing to his help, like a good Samaritan, with my friends, to arrange for the funeral of his father, who was living with him and had died suddenly, he showed no recognition of this fact and even seemed to avoid me when I happened to meet him much later. Of course I have no regrets as he was no friend of mine at any time.

N. P. Nabar and M. M. Lad were my contemporaries in the High Court. They were both under-studies with A. A. Adarkar, a senior Advocate. Nabar was brilliant but was a frustrated person. He had joined the High Court Bar, only in name. He did not seem to be keen on practice. He was a master of English and Sanskrit. He had studied astrology on the basis of original Sanskrit text. He had given me some predictions on my life and they proved to be quite correct. It may be, because of his knowledge about his own future, he had lost interest in life, and led a somewhat reckless life, which ultimately killed him. He had died during the summer vacation when I had gone to Belgaum. A brilliant and most promising life was thus cut short. I was very close to him and I felt extremely sad on learning of his demise. He used to make great fun of M. M. Lad, referring to him as the brother of I. C. S. P. M. Lad, as though he had no individuality of his own.

Lad was studious and quite serious about his work. We three formed a good company in the high court and outside. It was Lad who introduced me to Dr. A. R. Rangnekar, a modern 'Dhanwantari' when my wife was ill with some kidney trouble. We had tried other doctors, but they were not able to help her much. Dr. Rangnekar correctly diagnosed the disease, gave the correct treatment both curative and preventive in future. Dr. Rangnekar was our family doctor till he died, for nearly 30/35 years. Lad was kindly and helpful. We often met and discussed things generally. He joined Port Trust service and retired as a Deputy General Manager. He died a few years ago.

Nirmala Raje Bhonsale, Ranisaheb of Akkalkot, was one of our close family friends. We used to meet often either at our place in Worli or at her apartment in 'Akash Ganga' on Bhulabhai Desai Road. She had her flat on the 23rd floor of the building and had it fashioned and furnished as she desired — herself being an artist of repute. She had an exceedingly charming personality and had a rare combination of poise, grace and royal manners.

My wife and I had close relations with her. We were family friends. During Nagpur sessions, we along with Kanchanmala Raje Bhonsale, her first cousin, Ranisaheb of Nagpur, spent most of the spare time together, that with lunches and dinners in the Bhonsale palace, seeing pictures and other places of entertainment. She had an excellent library at home and I used to regularly borrow books from her. Sharada Mukherjee was another member of our small group. We used to meet periodically and have luncheons and dinners together. Last days of Nirmala Raje were bordering on the pathetic. She led a lonely life and probably suffered from it. We tried to persuade Sharada Mukherjee, and her own brother to take care of her and look after her. But they were also not in a position to do much in that regard. Eventually we succeeded in prevailing upon Kanchanmala to come and look after her which she did, sincerely and assiduously. When she died, we did the funeral services. It was somewhat tragic that she, who was the grand niece of Sayajirao Gaekwad of Baroda and Rani Saheb of Akkalkot, and later a minister of Govt. had to end her days in that way. But destiny is destiny. Nobody, great or small, can escape it.

B. P. Dalal, an I. C. S. was a charming person, at once social, open, with no I. C. S. reserve. I had close and intimate relations with him, because of our official position — he was the Law Secretary of the State Govt., being its legal draftsman. We had common interest in the work of the Legislature — principally legislation and other things. He was highly intelligent, got on very well with Ministers and members alike and was an extremely likable person. He had a rare gift of wit and humour. In the annual winter session of the Legislature in Nagpur, we used to be, together, whether in the Council Hall or in the circuit house in the Civil Lines. This made our friendship still closer and warmer. He was a part of our small circle of friends, to which I have made reference elsewhere. He died rather prematurely a few years back.

Balasaheb Belvi, though very much senior to me in age and practice, was a close friend of mine. Mrs. Belvi, Indirabai, was a gem of a person. She had developed an intimate friendship with my wife. Indeed, we two, were very close families. Belvi was well-read and well-informed and had a genuine sense of humour. But he was a bit easy going and therefore remained only a middle-level practitioner. He had potentiality and other equipment for a successful lawyer. If he had put both to proper use, he would have gone far ahead. But he had no regrets of any kind. His company was always entertaining, with his wit and humour. I still remember his witty observations on Dr. Jayaker, his neighbour Anikhindi and generally various men and matters. He died a few years ago. His wife had died a little earlier. He was completely at sea when his wife died, as most of us do. We, so much depend on our wives.

Gumaste, junior to me, was another close friend of ours. Gumastes were a great help to us. Senior Gumaste had acquired a large practice and built a prestigious building in Fort area, 'Dhannur' named after his native village. It was rare that one could build such a big building in the most prestigious area in Bombay. His stock went up automatically. Advocates, on the Appellate side, were a kind of orthodox people, were solid financially but made no great show of their wealth. In our time, only the Govt. Pleader kept a car, and everybody else commuted in a tram-car now abolished.

Junior Gumaste was a great help to my brother Appa. He gladly allowed him to use the top floor of his building 'Venktesh Bhavan' in Pune, when he had to serve in the Social Welfare Department of Govt. in Pune. It was his first appointment after his M.A. degree, from the well-known Institute of Social Sciences, Chembur in Bombay. He also helped him successfully in a high court case concerning a service matter. He remained a good friend throughout. He died very recently.

Balasaheb Lokur was another very close friend of ours. He was junior to me in the High Court. While he continued at the Bar, I was drafted into the High Court service, as a Dy. Registrar, on the Appellate side. We had become and have remained close family friends. They were a great help to me when my wife suddenly died in 1992. Mrs. Padma Lokur remained at our place till evening and did all phoning to our people, in India and abroad, to convey this sad news. Lokur, who had been a presidency magistrate, soon joined Govt. of India, as a Legal Advisor in the Law Ministry. He eventually became the head of the

Bombay Office of the Law Ministry and retired from there. He settled down in Bombay. We have been close family friends for several decades. My wife and myself were also equally friendly with her (Mrs. Padma Lokur's) sister Mrs. Kamal Pandit, and mother Ranisaheb of Bhor known to us as Amma. Recently his son Mukund had arranged a big party to celebrate his (Balasaheb's) completion of 80 years. I was specially invited for this but I could not make it. We kept on meeting whenever they came to Pune, or I went to Bombay. They have always been a source of strength to me, especially after my wife's death.

Ramrao Deshmukh and his wife Kamalini are also our family friends. Ramrao has now settled in Pune. We meet occasionally, though not often, whenever convenient. Probably we would have met more often, if my wife had been alive. She had a much better rapport with all our friends whether by meeting directly or on the phone. Ramrao and his wife Leenatai as she is known, have a great gift of collecting friends, in various fields viz. Art, Literature, Social and Cultural activities etc. He leads a very disciplined life, following his diverse interests in a systematic way. He is the last surviving brother of the famous Deshmukh family. His eldest brother was Chintamanrao Deshmukh, I.C.S., a great name in India and abroad. He has translated quite a few books from English into Marathi and vice-versa. He has translated into English (A Village Has No Walls) the celebrated book 'Banagarwadi' by Venktesh Madgulkar, now also made into a very popular film version. I cherish many happy memories of our meetings in his Bank-House residence in Bombay, on various occasions. One was at the time of a musical concert by Kumar Gandharva, at his residence, in celebration of completion of 80 years of his famous brother Chintamanrao. Another was when we were joined in our discussions by 'Anil' a well-known poet of Maharashtra and also his close relative, and Setu Madhavrao Pagadi, a great literary figure. Deshmukhs had really converted their house into a house of culture. He still continued to do so, at his Pune residence, until his tragic accidental death a little while ago.

N. Raghunathan, I.A.S., had become our family friend, right from the days of his Deputy Secretaryship— a young, dynamic person, well-versed in English and Sanskrit alike, at once affable and lovable, despite his high position in government. We were equally friendly with his parents who lived with him., His parents in-law also became our friends. His father-in-law Raj Gopal Ayyengar, had been a judge of the Supreme Court of India. He was equally affable and I visited him at his residence in New Delhi and also breakfasted with him, which was a full meal, whenever I went there for official work. He was then the Chairman of Press Council of India. Raj Gopal's health had become a cause of anxiety and worry to Raghunathan and my wife Padmavati, as usual went to his rescue and gave him great moral support, shared his anxiety and assured him that there was nothing to worry and he would be alright soon. So it happened also.

When a person is worried, some words of consolation and assurance and sharing his feelings in the matter goes a long way in assuaging his feelings and anxiety. My wife had the rare knack of entering into and sharing genuinely, the worries and anxieties of the person, which at once created conditions of confidence and assurance. I believe that this was how we became close family friends. His wife Shamala is equally affable and lovable. She is a noble lady with poise, grace and dignified bearing. They form a very happy family with their two children, Ashwin and Daya. Now both of them are happily married and are in U.S.A.

We had undertaken a memorable tour of South India, lasting for nearly 20 days or so. Daya and Ashwin were very young and Ashwin's "Jawal" i.e. first-time hair-cut was to be performed at Kumbhakonam. We journeyed throughout in a car. We visited Bangalore, Tanjawur, Kumbhakonam, Coimbatore, Guruwayur, forest areas in Mysore, Mysore and Shri Tirupati. It was a most enjoyable trip, covering a large number of places on the way like Salem, Krishnagiri, Trichenapalli, Namakkal and on our return we stayed for a while in Belgaum, Hukeri, Pune and then back to Bombay. We also visited Mahabaleshwar in their company with Shrinivasan and his wife Vatsala (Shamala's sister) joining us. I have many happy memories of our frequent meetings, spending hours together. My wife was at the beck and call whenever there was a need for it, may be Ashwin's illness or his father's demise after a short illness. We attended Daya's marriage at Madras as his guests and were looked after with every care and attention. We also visited Shri Tirupati, a visit arranged by him, during our stay there. Later we stopped at Delhi for a while on our way back from Shri Badrinath in 1992 and took an opportunity to visit them. Raghunathan was then the Secretary for the Defence Production in the Ministry of Defence of Government of India. It was 1 p.m. or 2 p.m. We intended to have a cup of tea only and return. But no, Shamala prepared food for us and we had a hearty meal at their residence. Raghunathan had come home during lunch-break. We chatted for some time and started to return. Raghunathan lent his car after reaching him at his office and we were back at our place. This was real hospitality, epitomizing our great ancient culture and tradition. He retired recently as the Chief Secretary to Maharashtra Government and has settled down at his Worli residence in Bombay. I am always assured of a warm and loving welcome and hospitality whenever I happen to visit his place.

Vishram Bedekar, a great literary figure of Maharashtra, was a new acquisition in friendship. When we moved to 'Dinath Court' in Worli, in 1970, Bedekars — Vishram and his equally erudite wife Malatibai, were our neighbours, on the 2nd floor, while we were on the third floor. Bedekars were not easily communicable. Indeed we did not meet, until the siren of 'Blackout' was sounded and we all gathered together on the ground floor. But afterwards, we became close family friends. Their company was always interesting and entertaining. I have many happy memories of our meetings and illuminating discussions.

Once he took me out, in his car, and we visited a few places together, saw some exhibitions at Nariman Point, had lunch together in the canteen of Jehangir Art Gallery and returned home in the evening. He also took us to the premier show of his play — 'Tilak and Agarkar' which he had written, directed and produced. Miss Leela Desai, the well-known dancer and actress of bygone days, was also with us. She too had become our family friend, and we met quite a few times, at her place in 'Shandilya' in Worli. When she left her flat and decided to settle down in Calcutta/Jamshedpur she stayed with us for a few days. She was an exceedingly nice woman, loving and hospitable; I had seen the film 'President' where she acted as the heroine, with the great Saigal as the hero. She was good enough to take us to that picture, when it was shown in a mini-theatre on Marine Lines.

When I was ill in the hospital, at the time of operation for "prostate" Bedekar visited me there and helped us in many ways, and was a great source of strength to us. They moved to Pune where they are being looked after by persons arranged by Shrikant, their only son. After moving to Pune, after my wife's death, I used to visit them off and on. He died recently after a short illness. He had read the manuscript of my book, 'Practice and Procedure in Indian Legislatures', not his subject, and made careful notes in his small handwriting. I was greatly beholden to him for this kindness and concern for me. The book was later on printed and published by the well-known firm of publishers N. M. Tripathi & Co.

N. R. Rao and his wife Malati became our family friends because of our common interest in the activities of 'Satya Dhyana' Vidyapeeth at Mulund. We used to attend weekly 'Bhajans' — devotional songs, at 'Vani-Vihar Vidyalaya' in Matunga every Thursday evening. Rao used to take us, in his car, from our residence at Worli and reach us back to our door. This, he did without fail till I left Bombay to settle in Pune. He was a great help to us in every way. We have undertaken many visits together, arranged by him viz. Badrinath, Tirupati, Mantralayam and Udipi. Unfortunately all this happened after my wife's death, except perhaps in the case of Shri Tirupati when my wife was still with us. I used to play tennis with Mrs. Rao, quite often, on the courts of Bombay

Gymkhana. Mrs. Rao was a crack player and used to play excellent tennis, clad in Indian sari. Rao also helped me a great deal at the time of leaving Bombay— in Bank matters and other things. I was instrumental in securing his services, for our Poorna Pragna Education centre at Dahisar, where he did his work meticulously, not sparing his health, which had suffered in the process. Somehow he and Swamiji differed on some occasions but he always stuck to his position which was not liked by Swamiji. He left the centre at his own request, on health grounds.

I am fortunate in having friends like him and this has sustained me in my old age.

Chapter XII

CONCLUSION

I continued to live in Bombay, after my wife's demise, for about 2 years or so. I was not able to arrange things to my satisfaction for a comfortable life there. Everything was on an improvised basis. Meanwhile pressure was building on me to move to Pune since my brother Appa, sister Indu (Mrs. Dhumale) and Vijayarao Chebbi, my sister's son-in-law and others did not like my staying alone in Bombay. The landlord also was inducing me to surrender the flat to him, and nobody else, if I decided to move to Pune. The cumulative effect of all this, resulted in my finally deciding to leave Bombay and settle in Pune. Things then moved quickly. I left Bombay some time in March 1994. I felt a wrench in my heart to leave Bombay, where I had lived and worked for 60 years. Probably I would never have left Bombay if my wife had not died then. But destiny has always its own plans and eventually I opted for Pune. Since to cut off all my relation with Bombay, was something I could not stomach, I purchased a small one bed-room flat in Worli, intending to visit Bombay for 3/4 days—every month or even every two months. This, I did for a couple of years.

I succeeded in securing a good spacious flat in Pune, in Himali Housing Complex, built by Naralkar. Actually

I moved in my flat after completing the formalities in June 1994. Since then I have been living there. It is a nice complex, with facilities like a swimming pool, health club, with up to date equipment and social club for recreation and entertainment. In the beginning, I was the informal President, elected by a general body of the residents and I worked as such for about 3 years till we were able to persuade Naralkar to grant us all, our membership and share certificates. Now a regular society is functioning under Major Shah as its President, and about 5 others as the members of the Managing Committee, all duly elected as required by law.

How has been my life, here in Pune, in the new surroundings? I have been able to secure help, by way of a cook and a maid-servant to do washing, cleaning etc. But I have not been quite happy about the arrangements. Things were not as easy as I had thought. Pune is equally difficult in the matter of servants. This went on for some time. My maid-servant has however continued to work with me after my cook left and she started cooking also, which she learnt in the meanwhile. Since some time, her son has been with me and is useful to do some odd jobs. I have now arrangements, fairly satisfactory so far as actual living is concerned. But, I am missing my Bombay life and the various activities. I am missing my club life particularly, Bombay Gymkhana where I have been a member for the last many years. I still continue to be so.

Pune is known for its healthy climate. But latterly due to influx of people and rapid and haphazard expansion, it is no longer what it was a few years ago. Its climate also has undergone a change, being now very hot in summer and severely cold in winter. Only monsoon is good, with a small rainfall, with English like weather as the British used to say. Life also is as expensive as in Bombay — perhaps even more expensive. Here, people seem to think that we have all come here, only to pay them as much as they want.

Traffic conditions are atrocious. It is difficult, if not impossible, to cross a road, with vehicles of all sorts—specially two wheelers, scooters etc. rushing from both sides, disregarding traffic rules. Pune climate has not suited me, since I am used to Bombay climate, which is neither too hot, nor too cold, with not great difference between maximum and minimum temperatures. I have not been able to keep my health as well as in Bombay. Apart from the weather, there was either over-medication or wrong medication for minor ailments like cold and cough. My system is not used to drugs at all. Administration of strong drugs like antibiotics for minor ailments, has had its adverse effects. But destiny has brought me here and I must try to live as best as I can. I have always believed that whatever happens, happens for the good. But I am not unhappy. I have here also a good circle of warm and helpful friends and I have been able to lead a fairly happy and comfortable life. My relatives come and meet me often, and I do not feel quite lonely, as might have been the case in Bombay. I could, without any difficulty, stay with my brother Appa if I so chose or if it becomes necessary. They have always welcomed me and I am sure of every help and care to make my stay comfortable if I choose to live with them. But, as of now, I have opted to live in my own place and follow my way of life.

I have not planned my life in any respect, whether it is education in any particular discipline or service—

career of any kind or for the matter of that life in retirement. I have always accepted things as they have happened and I have no regrets of any kind in the matter. We plan and fail while destiny has its own plan and it works accordingly. I am now truly convinced of what 'Geeta' teaches us: 'I am not the doer but only an instrument in the hands of 'Parameshwar,' the Almighty who does everything.' What is true of an individual is also true of the nation. We are only expected to do our duty in the allotted fields, and we should do it well, leaving everything in the hands of the Almighty God. This is a sound precept both in theory and practice. Life is a mixture of good and bad, like the *proverbial curate's* egg, good in parts and bad in others. This is also the beauty of life which makes it for its sweetness and worth. One however feels that one could have done much more. I am only tempted to refer to Robert Browning's philosophical poem "The *last* side together". In that, he says that one is never able to achieve all, one wants to achieve and one should be satisfied with whatever one has been able to achieve. Hence his dictum — petty done, and vast undone. Then why grieve?

I have served my parents and other members of the family as best as I could, with my late brother Dr. Krishna, lending a big helping hand. I see now all my family members and their progeny well-settled in life and even prospering in a big way.

Appendix I

GENEALOGY

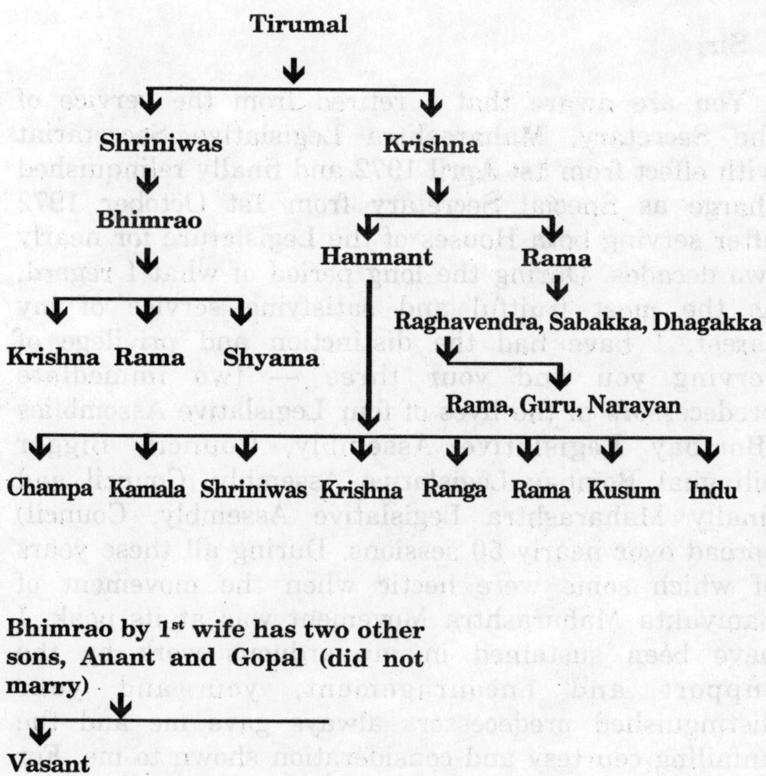

APPENDIX II

Poona,
5th December 1972

To
The Honourable Speaker/Chairman,
Maharashtra Legislative Assembly,
Camp Nagpur.

Sir,

You are aware that I retired from the service of the Secretary, Maharashtra Legislative Secretariat with effect from 1st April 1972 and finally relinquished charge as Special Secretary from 1st October 1972 after serving both Houses of the Legislature for nearly two decades. During the long period of what I regard, as the most fruitful and satisfying service of my career, I have had the distinction and privilege of serving you and your three — two immediate predecessors in the lives of four Legislative Assemblies (Bombay Legislative Assembly, Council, Bigger bilingual Bombay Legislative Assembly, Council and finally Maharashtra Legislative Assembly, Council) spread over nearly 50 sessions. During all these years of which some were hectic when the movement of Samyukta Maharashtra Movement was at its peak, I have been sustained in my arduous work by the support and encouragement, you and your distinguished predecessors always gave me and the unfailing courtesy and consideration shown to me. For all this I am indeed grateful. To the members of the House, past and present, my profuse thanks are due, which I extend unreservedly for their ready and willing cooperation in all that, I, as its servant, endeavoured to do in the service of the House. My work was made not only easier but pleasanter because of the utmost kindness, cordiality and friendliness shown to me by one and all of them.

I must also express my grateful thanks to the Honourable Ministers — notably the Honourable Chief Ministers (past and present) who readily appreciated my difficulties and extended to me in abundant measure their cooperation and help, even though I am conscious, I might have annoyed them on certain occasions but they all knew it was all in the service of the House.

I cannot forget my brother officers and other members of the staff high and low (who were my real sinews) who not only gave me the utmost cooperation during many trying and difficult periods — they gave me much more — their love and affection, which enabled me to work in the organisation as one family. I am really proud of them all.

Lastly I must also place on record my thanks to my brother officers — both in this country and abroad — wherever I was privileged to go on delegation and in conferences for the ready welcome and friendliness with which they overwhelmed me.

I now leave the field with great regret but not without many happy memories and the sense of satisfaction of contributing something, howsoever small, in the building up of parliamentary democracy, which is so dear to all of us.

I beg to remain, Sir,

Yours faithfully,
(S. H. Belavadi)

APPENDIX III

Extracts from Maharashtra Legislative Assembly

(Official Gazette) Vol. 38, Sr. No. 26 -

Friday, the 7th September 1973

श्री. वसंतराव नाईक (मुख्यमंत्री)

'...सचिवाचे काम हे नेहमीच कठीण असते. अनेकदा राज्यकर्त्या पक्षाला किंवा विरोधी पक्षाला सुद्धा त्यांच्याकडून वागणूक बरोबर मिळत नाही अशा तऱ्हेची तक्रार करण्याकरिता पुष्कळदा वाव असण्याची शक्यता असते. या सभागृहाची प्रतिष्ठा वाढावी व या सभागृहाचे कामकाज चांगल्या तऱ्हेने व नियमाला धरून चालवावे लागत असल्यामुळे त्यासाठी कठोर निर्णय त्यांना घ्यावे लागतात व तसा सल्ला द्यावा लागतो. सल्ला देण्याचे जे कठीण काम असते ते करण्याची पाळी पुष्कळवेळा सचिवावर येत असते. हे काम गेली १९ वर्षे श्री. बेलवडी यांनी अत्यंत तडफेने व मनाची स्थिरता कायम ठेवून केले आहे. सभागृहाच्या कामकाजाबद्दल कोणी काही तक्रार केली तर त्याबाबत समजूत पटवून देण्याचेही काम त्यांनी केले आहे. त्यांनी केलेल्या कामाबद्दलचे कौतुक सर्व सभासद करतील याबद्दल माझ्या मनात शंका नाही. तेव्हा अशा तऱ्हेचे १९ वर्षे हे कठीण असणारे काम त्यांनी केले व त्यामध्ये ते यशस्वी झाले म्हणून ते रिटायर्ड झाल्यानंतरही त्यांना रिएम्प्लॉय केले होते व यामध्येच त्यांच्या पसंतीची पावती आहे.'

श्री. दि. बा. पाटील (पनवेल)

'....सभागृहाचे कामकाज पार पाडीत असताना वेळप्रसंगी सत्तारुढ पक्षाची नाराजी जरी पत्करावी लागली तरी त्याला ते तयार असत. त्यांची कर्तव्यतत्परता आम्ही वेळोवेळी बघितली आहे. त्यांनी आपल्या पत्रांत उल्लेख केल्याप्रमाणे संयुक्त महाराष्ट्राच्या चळवळीच्या काळात या सभागृहाच्या बैठका ज्यावेळी भरत असत त्यावेळी त्या अतिशय तंग परिस्थितीमध्ये भरत असत आणि अशा तंग परिस्थितीमध्ये सभापतींना सभागृहाचे कामकाज नियमाला धरून कसे चालवावे, याचे मार्गदर्शन करण्याचा ते प्रयत्न करीत असत. अनेक वेळा आम्हा विरोधकांना देखील त्यांची सल्लामसलत व मदत घ्यावी लागली आहे. लोकशाहीचे हे कर्तव्य बजावीत असताना निःपक्षपातीपणाने त्यांनी ते बजाविले आहे व सभागृहाची प्रतिष्ठा चांगली व कायम राहावी याची त्यांना सतत जाणीव होती.'

श्री. रा. का. म्हाळगी (शुक्रवार पेठ)

'श्री. बेलवडींच्या संबंधी हे म्हणता येईल की, नियमाला धरून कामकाज चालले पाहिजे असा त्यांचा विशेष आग्रह असायचा, आणि त्यांनी तो आग्रह काटेकोरपणे पाळायचा प्रयत्नही केला. या विधानमंडळ सचिवालयात ते गेली १९ वर्षे होते. त्यांच्या बाबतीतील एक गोष्ट खरी आहे की, त्यांना त्यांचा आग्रह पार पाडीत असताना काही लोकांना दुखवावे लागले आहे, हे आम्ही आमच्या डोळ्यांनी पाहिले आहे. सत्तारुढ पक्षाला कधी दुखवावे लागत असे, तर कधी आम्हालाही दुखवावे लागत असे. परंतु, शेवटी त्यांच्या मनात आमच्याविषयी काही निराळी भावना आहे असा प्रसंग कधी आला नाही.'

'...लेजिस्लेटरने पार्लमेंटरी डिव्हाइसेस चांगल्या प्रकारे कसे वापरावेत यासंबंधी त्यांनी मार्गदर्शन केले आहे. ज्यावेळी आमच्यापैकी काही सदस्य नियमानुसार कामकाज चालविण्याच्या पद्धतीतून पार्लमेंटरी डिव्हाइसेस योग्य वेळी वापरीत असत, त्यावेळी सभागृहाच्या बाहेर त्याचा उल्लेखही त्यांनी केला आहे.'

श्रीमती मृणाल गोरे (मालाड)

'....सचिव म्हणून त्यांनी निःपक्षपातीपणे कामगिरी बजाविली असल्याचे माझ्या सहकाऱ्याकडून मी ऐकले आहे. माझा त्यांचा संबंध अलिकडचा असला तरी माझ्या पूर्वीच्या सहकाऱ्यांचे त्यांच्याबाबतचे मत मला माहीत आहे. श्री. बेलवडी हे निःपक्षपातीपणे या सभागृहाचा कारभार चालविण्यास मदत करीत असत. या राज्याचे मुख्यमंत्री सभागृहात बसले असतानाही राज्यकर्त्या पक्षाकडून काही सूचना आल्या व त्या नियमात बसत नसल्या, तर त्या नियमात बसत नाहीत असे सांगण्याचे धारिष्ट्य जे सचिवाजवळ असावयास पाहिजे तसे धारिष्ट्य श्री बेलवडी यांच्याकडे भरपूर होते. म्हणूनच या विधिमंडळाच्या ज्या परंपरा आहेत त्या जोपासण्याचा व कामकाज नियमानुसार चालविण्याचा काटेकोरपणा ते तत्परतेने करू शकले.'

श्री. वानखेडे, अध्यक्ष

'.... त्यानंतर जवळ जवळ १५-१६ वर्षे मी या राज्यामध्ये मंत्री म्हणून काम करीत असताना आणि विशेषतः कायदामंत्री म्हणून या ठिकाणी काम करण्याचा ज्यावेळी प्रसंग आला त्यावेळी नियमांना धरून कार्य करण्याची त्यांची पद्धत आणि संसदीय राज्यपद्धती कशी काय चालवावी, या दृष्टीकोनातून त्यांनी केलेला सखोल अभ्यास या दोहोंचा अनुभव माझ्या प्रत्ययास आला.' '.... एवढेच नव्हे तर देशामध्ये जेवढ्या विधानसभा आहेत, व त्या विधानसेभेचे जे जे सचिव आहेत, त्यांच्यामध्ये श्री. बेलवडींचे विशेष असे स्थान होते. ज्यावेळी विशिष्ट कामासाठी देशाचा प्रतिनिधी म्हणून कोठेही प्रतिनिधीत्व करण्याचा प्रसंग येई त्यावेळी मध्यवर्ती सचिवालयाकडून सुद्धा श्री. बेलवडींचे पुष्कळदा त्या कामासाठी सिलेक्शन झालेले होते. जगामध्ये त्या निमित्ताने न्यूझिलंड, ऑस्ट्रेलिया, इंग्लंड व त्यानंतर शेवटी शेवटी फ्रान्स या देशात संसदीय पद्धतीचे विशिष्ट शिक्षण घेण्यासाठी ते गेले होते. त्यांच्या अनुभवांनी त्यांनी या ठिकाणी ज्या विशेष पद्धती घालून दिल्या होत्या त्यांचा अवलंब या सचिवालयामध्ये आजही केला जात आहे.'

APPENDIX IV

Extracts from Maharashtra Legislative Council

(Official Gazette) Vol. 38, Sr. No. 26 -

Friday the 7th September 1973

श्री उ. ल. पाटील, महाराष्ट्र पदवीधर

'... मी या सभागृहाचा सभासद सन १९५४ पूर्वीही होतो. त्यानंतर मी लोकसभेत निवडून आल्यानंतर तसा श्री. बेलवडी यांच्याशी दैनंदिन संबंध जरी आला नसला तरी ते निरनिराळ्या वेळी दिल्लीला येत असत. विशेषतः उपविधान समितीच्या बैठकीच्या निमित्ताने किंवा इतर निमित्ताने त्यांची आणि माझी जेव्हा जेव्हा दिल्लीला भेट झाली त्या त्या वेळी त्यांच्याशी माझे संसदीय कामकाजासंबंधी बोलणे झाले. त्यावरून मला या ठिकाणी मोकळेपणाने कबूल करावयास हरकत नाही, की श्री. बेलवडी यांचा संसदीय कामकाजाच्या बाबतीत महाराष्ट्र विधानसभेत आणि इतत्रही फार मोलाचा हिस्सा राहिला आहे. या सभागृहाचा सभासद या नात्याने सभासदांना जे हक्क असतात त्यासंबंधी श्री. बेलवडी हे अतिशय जागरुक असत व सभासदांना त्यांच्या हक्काची जाणीव करून देण्याचे काम त्यांनी जाणीवपूर्वक केले आहे. मला याही गोष्टीची पूर्ण कल्पना आहे की महाराष्ट्राच्या विधिमंडळात विरोधी पक्षाला हळूहळू का होईना, परंतु मान्यता प्राप्त करून देण्यासाठी व विरोधी पक्षाचा दर्जा वाढविण्यासाठी श्री. बेलवडी यांनी शासनाची मनोभूमिका तयार करण्याची प्रक्रिया केली व आज येथे विरोधी पक्षांना जो दर्जा व मान्यता आहे त्यात श्री. बेलवडी यांचा वाटा मोठा आहे. जेव्हा जेव्हा विधिमंडळाच्या कामकाजात काही पेच प्रसंग निर्माण झाले तेव्हा तेव्हा जगातील देशांच्या विधिमंडळात असे प्रसंग निर्माण झाले असताना कोणती भूमिका घेण्यात आली होती यासंबंधीचा रेडी रेफरन्स श्री. बेलवडी यांच्यापाशी असावयाचा

आणि पेचप्रसंगातून मार्ग निघावयाचा एवढा त्यांचा संसदीय कामाचा जबर अभ्यास होता. मला स्वतःला असे वाटते की, संसदेत ज्याप्रमाणे संसद सचिवांनी गौरवपर कामगिरी केल्यानंतर राज्यसभेत नामनियुक्त सभासद म्हणून त्यांना घेण्याची पद्धत सुरू केली आहे. त्याचप्रमाणे येथे श्री. बेलवडी यांना जर विधानपरिषदेत नामनियुक्त सभासद म्हणून घेतले गेले तर सभागृहाचा मोठा फायदा होईल. विधिमंडळाच्या कामकाजाच्या दृष्टीने ही गोष्ट हितकारक ठरणार असल्यामुळे माझ्या या सूचनेचा पुढे तरी शासनाने विचार करावा अशी मी विनंती करतो. अध्यक्ष महाराज, श्री. बेलवडींचे कार्य आणखी एका दृष्टीने प्रशंसनीय आहे. नवीन सभासद निवडून आल्यावर संसदीय कामकाजाची त्यांना माहिती व्हावी या हेतूने कॉमनवेल्थ पार्लमेंटरी असोसिएशनतर्फे सभासदांसाठी प्रशिक्षण वर्ग जे सुरू करण्यात आले ते सुरू करण्यात त्यांचा वाटा फार मोठा होता. सभासदांनी विधिमंडळाच्या कामकाजात रस घ्यावा, हे काम करीत असताना स्वतःचाही बौद्धिक विकास साधावा, या दृष्टीने या प्रशिक्षण वर्गाचा फायदा होतो. कॉमनवेल्थ पार्लमेंटरी असोसिएशनचे काम श्री. बेलवडी यांनी अत्यंत चांगल्या प्रकारे चालविले आणि महत्वाची गोष्ट अशी की, सी.पी.ए. च्या वतीने वेगवेगळ्या विचारसरणीच्या काही सभासदांना परदेशात जाऊन तेथील विधिमंडळाचे काम कसे चालते, हे पाहण्याची संधीही मिळावी. याकरिता श्री. बेलवडी यांनी प्रयत्न केले आणि अनुकूल वातावरण निर्माण केले. सचिव म्हणून श्री. बेलवडी यांची प्रदीर्घ अशी कारकीर्द झाली आहे.

श्री. ना. ज्ञा. पाटील, विधानसभेने निवडलेले

'.... १९५७ ते १९६२ या काळात खालच्या सभागृहात ११ अनेक प्रसंग निर्माण झाले; परंतु त्या प्रसंगी श्री. बेलवडी यांनी अत्यंत समतोलपणे अध्यक्षांना सल्ला दिला व अत्यंत बिकट अशा कालखंडातही मनाचा समतोल ढळू न देता निर्णय घेण्यासाठी मनाची जी अवस्था लागते, कुवत लागते ती त्यांच्यापाशी होती असे याठिकाणी निश्चितपणे मान्य केले पाहिजे. सभागृहातील सदस्यांना मार्गदर्शनपर असे महत्त्वाचे लिखाण श्री. बेलवडी यांनी केले आहे. विधिमंडळ सचिवालयाच्यावतीने 'पर्लमेंटरी टॉपिक्स' या नावाने

त्यांच्या लिखाणाचे जे पुस्तक प्रसिद्ध झाले त्याचा सभासदांना चांगला उपयोग झाला आहे. सभासदांचे हक्क कोणते, कोणत्या मार्गाने जनतेच्या जिव्हाळ्याचे प्रश्न सभागृहात उपस्थित करता येतात, याचे मार्गदर्शन त्यांनी नेहमी केले.'

श्री. ग. प्र. प्रधान

'... विधिमंडळाच्या सचिवांना आपल्या अधिकाराची कक्षा सांभाळावयाची आणि लोकशाहीच्या आशयाचे रक्षण करावयाचे, अशा दोन्ही गोष्टी पार पाडावयाच्या असतात. अशा वेळी या अधिकाऱ्याचं काम अनेक वेळा कठीण असते. शासनाची भूमिका एक असते, विरोधी पक्षाची भूमिका एक असते अशा वेळी निःपक्षपातीपणे आणि विधिमंडळाची इभ्रत उंचावण्याच्या दृष्टीने सल्ला देणे हे आपले कर्तव्य त्यांनी चांगल्या रितीने बजाविले. कै. कृष्णाजी प्रभाकर खाडिलकर यांच्या नाटकातील ज्योतिषी राजाच्या डोळ्यांकडे पाहून भविष्य सांगत असतो. परंतु श्री. बेलवडी यांनी राज्यकर्त्यांच्या डोळ्यांकडे पाहून निर्णय दिला नाही, सल्ला दिला नाही. विरोधी पक्षाच्या अधिकारांचा संकोच होऊ नये म्हणून ते जागृत राहिले. कॉमनवेल्थ पार्लमेंटरी असोसिएशनच्या महाराष्ट्र शाखेतर्फे नवीन सदस्यांना मार्गदर्शन करण्यासाठी वर्ग भरविले जात असतात. अशा वर्गात त्यांनी सदस्यांना बहुमोल मार्गदर्शन केले. अशा प्रकारे नवीन सदस्यांना मार्गदर्शन करणारे अधिकारी क्वचितच मिळू शकतात. निरनिराळ्या समित्यांकडून त्यांचे समित्यांच्या अध्यक्षांना आणि सदस्यांना सहाय्य होत असे. समित्यांमधील त्यांच्या कामात रेखीवपणा असे आणि तपशिलात ग्रीप असते. या समित्यांच्या कामकाजातून सत्यशोधन व्हावे असा त्यांचा कटाक्ष असे. ते विधिमंडळाचे सचिव म्हणून निवृत्त होत असले, तरी वेगळ्या रितीने त्यांचा उपयोग करून घेता येतो काय, हे पाहिले पाहिजे.

उपसभापती

'.... सभागृहापुढील प्रस्तावात ज्या भावना व्यक्त करण्यात आल्या आहेत त्यांच्याशी तर मी सहमत आहेच; परंतु श्री. बेलवडी यांनी आपल्या सेवेने आणि कार्याने संसदीय कामकाजाच्या प्रथांत जी महत्त्वाची भर घातली त्यांचा या ठिकाणी संक्षिप्त रूपाने उल्लेख करणे माझे कर्तव्य आहे असे मला वाटते.

संसदीय प्रथा शिकविणे ही गोष्ट वेगळी आहे आणि संसदीय प्रथांशी समरस होणे ही गोष्ट वेगळी आहे. श्री. बेलवडी यांनी संसदीय कामकाज आणि संसदीय प्रथा यांविषयी पुस्तक लिहिणे वेगळे आणि त्यांनी संसदीय प्रथा जोपासणे, त्यांची वाढ करणे वेगळे. या दोन्ही गोष्टी त्यांनी समर्थपणे केल्या आहेत. श्री. बेलवडी हे संसदीय प्रथांचे चालते-बोलते पुस्तकच होते. श्री. बेलवडी म्हणजे पार्लमेंटरी प्रोसीजरचे, 'मेज पार्लमेंटरी प्रॅक्टिसचे' सहा फुट उंचीचे पुस्तक होते असे मी म्हटले तर त्यात अतिशयोक्ती होणार नाही. पार्लमेंटरी प्रोसीजरची जी पुस्तके आहेत त्यांचे श्री. बेलवडी म्हणजे एक डायजेस्ट होते असे म्हटले तरी चालेल. त्यांनी आपल्या कारकिर्दीत अनेक संसदीय प्रथांची भर घातली. त्यांना ज्या सूचना किंवा प्रथा योग्य वाटत त्या ते विरोधी पक्षासमोर, मंत्र्यासमोर मांडीत असत. संसदीय समित्यांचा अध्यक्ष हा मंत्री असू नये अशी प्रथा पाडण्याचा प्रयत्न करण्यात मंत्र्यांची नाराजी पत्करण्याचा धोका असतानाही त्यांनी ती प्रथा रुढ करण्याचा प्रयत्न केला. आपल्या येथे लोकलेखा समितीचा अध्यक्ष हा विरोधी पक्षातील असतो. ही प्रथा पाडण्याचे श्रेय श्री. बेलवडी यांना आहे. लोकशाहीत विरोधी पक्ष नेत्याला मंत्र्याइतकाच दर्जा असावा या दृष्टीने त्यांनी मौलिक स्वरूपाच्या सूचना केल्या. विरोधी पक्षाला लोकशाहीत शॅडो गर्व्हनमेंट समजले जाते. दुर्दैवाने म्हणा अगर सुदैवाने म्हणा, पर्यायी सत्ताधारी पक्ष म्हणून महाराष्ट्रातील विरोधी पक्ष कितपत सबल आहे ही गोष्ट वेगळी. परंतु या राज्यात विरोधी पक्ष नेत्याला मंत्र्याचा दर्जा असावा हा दृष्टीकोन श्री. बेलवडी यांनी हिरीरीने मांडला. संसदीय प्रथा अमलात आणण्याच्या दृष्टीने त्यांच्या अनेक कल्पना होत्या, त्या अद्याप अंमलात आलेल्या नाहीत. त्यांची नोंद सभागृहाच्या नेत्यांनी घ्यावी, तसेच महाराष्ट्रात विधिमंडळ सचिवालयाची स्वायतत्ता अबाधित ठेवावी असे मला वाटते.''

'.... दुसरी गोष्ट म्हणजे, शासनाने आपल्या अधिकाऱ्यांसाठी ॲडमिनिस्ट्रेटिव्ह कोर्सेस सुरू केले आहेत, कायदा खात्याच्या अधिकाऱ्यांसाठी प्रशिक्षण वर्ग सुरू केले आहेत. त्याप्रमाणे विधिमंडळाच्या अधिकाऱ्यांना संसदीय कामकाजाचे शिक्षण देण्यासाठीही एखादी संस्था असावी अशी त्यांची चिंता होती.'

APPENDIX V

Extracts from the Book
'History of Maharashtra Legislature'
by S. H. Belavadi & S. R. Kharabe
Shri P. K. Atre (page 121)

'उत्तरेकडून भारतावर जे संकट आले आहे त्या प्रकारचे संकट या देशावर येईल अशी स्वप्नातदेखील कोणाला कल्पना नव्हती. ज्या हिमालयाने भारतवर्षाचे अनंतकाळपर्यंत संरक्षण केले तो हिमालयच आज संकटात सापडावा आणि ज्याने आमचे संरक्षण केले त्याचे रक्षण करण्यासाठी आम्हाला धावत जाण्याची आज पाळी यावी, हा इतिहासाचा एक विलक्षण योगायोग आहे. महाराष्ट्राच्या मुख्यमंत्र्यांना संरक्षणमंत्री म्हणून राष्ट्राने जी हाक दिली आहे ती एक इतिहासाची हाक आहे, याबद्दल आम्हाला अतिशय आनंद होत आहे. या भारताचे रक्षण करण्याचा आम्हा मराठी लोकांचा हजारो वर्षांचा प्रघात आणि वारसा चालत आलेला असून त्या वारशाला शेवटी भारत सरकारला मान्यता द्यावी लागून महाराष्ट्राच्या मुख्यमंत्र्यांना आज हाक मारावी लागली, ही अतिशय आनंदाची गोष्ट आहे.

Shri P. K. Atre (page 124 & 126) :

'अध्यक्ष महाराज, पंडित नेहरू आपल्या जीवनामध्ये जेवढे मोठे आम्हाला दिसले त्याच्यापेक्षा ही सहस्त्रपटीने मोठे ते मृत्यूनंतर आढळून आले आहेत. जगामध्ये अनेक लोक होऊन गेले आणि त्यांच्या मृत्यूबद्दल अनेकांनी दुःख व्यक्त केले आहे. आपण जर जगाच्या इतिहासाचा थोडा अभ्यास केला,

तर आपल्याला दिसून येईल की, पंडित नेहरूंच्या निधनानिमित्ताने जगात जे दुःख व्यक्त करण्यात आले अशा प्रकारचे दुःख कोणाच्याही मृत्यूमुळे व्यक्त करण्यात आले नाही. अध्यक्ष महाराज, आपल्या पुराणातील कल्पनेप्रमाणे आपल्या देशात कोणतीही मोठी घटना घडली म्हणजे ३३ कोटी देव पुष्पवृष्टी करीत असत, परंतु पंडित नेहरूंच्या निधनामुळे ३०० कोटी लोकांनी पुष्पवृष्टी केली आहे. ते फक्त राष्ट्रपुरुषच होते असे नाही, तर ते युगपुरुष होते ही गोष्ट आपल्याला विसरून चालणार नाही.'

अध्यक्ष महाराज, युद्धमुक्त जग हे पंडित नेहरूंचे स्वप्न होते, किंबहुना ते त्यांचे जीवनध्येय होते आणि युद्धमुक्त जग हेच पंडितजींच्या स्मृतीचे चिरंतन स्मारक होऊ शकेल, दुसरे-तिसरे काहीही नाही. ज्या क्षणी जग खऱ्या अर्थाने युद्धमुक्त होईल तेव्हाच पंडितजींच्या विश्वशांतीसाठी तळमळणाऱ्या आत्म्याला शांती लाभेल, अन्यथा नाही. पंडितजींच्या या विश्वबंधुत्ववादी मनोवृत्तीमुळेच त्यांचे नाव अमेरिकेचे दिवंगत राष्ट्राध्यक्ष केनेडी, रशियाचे क्रुश्चेव्ह, इजिप्तचे नासर अथवा चीनचे माओत्सेतुंग यांच्या बरोबरीने जगाच्या राजकारणात घेतले जात असे.

जनतेच्या हृदयसिंहासनावरील त्यांचे स्थान अद्वितीय असेच होते. त्यांच्यासारखा लोकप्रिय नेता या देशात दुसरा कोणीही झालेला नाही. त्यांचे स्मरण आपण अहोरात्र करीत आहोत व पुढच्या शेकडो पिढ्या करीत राहतील. स्वातंत्र्याचे लढवय्ये, मानवतेचे पुजारी, भारताचे भाग्यविधाते अशा अनेक नात्यांनी ते आज आपणापुढे उभे आहेत. प्रख्यात कवी हरीन्द्रनाथ चट्टोपाध्याय यांनी आपल्या एका कवितेत म्हटले आहे की, यापुढे उगवणारा प्रत्येक दिवस हा छातीवर गुलाबाचे फुल लावून उगवेल आणि आपल्याला पंडित नेहरूंची आठवण करून देईल.

Shri P. K. Atre (Page 127) :

'आम्हाला नेहरूमध्ये भारताची प्रतिमा दिसते, त्यांच्या ओठावर आम्हाला गंगा यमुनांच्या लाटा दिसतात, तर त्यांच्या कपाळावर आम्हाला हिमालयाची भव्यता दिसते. मानवाच्या जीवनात जे जे म्हणून उज्ज्वल आहे, ऊर्जस्वल आहे, ते ते आम्हाला पंडित नेहरूंच्या व्यक्तिमत्वात पाहावयास मिळाले.

'ज्ञानेश्वरी'त म्हटल्याप्रमाणे : 'चंद्रमे जो अलांछन, मार्तण्ड जो तापहीन' असे त्यांचे व्यक्तिमत्व होते. हिमालयासारखा उत्तुंग, गंगेसारखा विशाल आणि पवित्र, गुलाबाच्या फुलांसारखा सुंदर व सुगंधमय असा महापुरुष या भारतवर्षात पुन्हा होणे शक्य नाही. मनुष्य जास्तीत जास्त किती महान होऊ शकतो यासंबंधीचा एक प्रयोग पंडित नेहरूंच्या द्वारे विधात्याने केला आणि तो प्रयोग पूर्णपणे यशस्वी झाला, असाच निर्वाळा इतिहासाला द्यावा लागेल.'

Shri Y. B. Chavan (page 122) :

'आज या सभागृहातून बाहेर पडताना माझ्या मनांत स्वतःबद्दल आत्मविश्वास जरूर आहे. परंतु ज्या बुजऱ्या मनाने मी या सभागृहात प्रवेश केला होता त्याच बुजऱ्या मनाने अधिक विशाल क्षेत्रामध्ये या संकटकाळात मी प्रवेश करणार आहे. अध्यक्ष महाराज, या सभागृहातील प्रत्येक गोष्टीवर, प्रत्येक वस्तूवर माझे प्रेम आहे. येथे झालेले वाद, येथे झालेल्या चर्चा, येथे झालेली भाषणे, येथे येऊन माझ्यावर रागावून बोलणारी, प्रेमाने बोलणारी माणसे या सर्वांवर माझे प्रेम आहे. लोकशाहीवर प्रेम करणाऱ्या मनुष्याच्या मनात असे प्रेम निर्माण होणे स्वाभाविक आहे असे मला वाटते. नव्या नव्हाळीचे प्रेम जसे उत्कट असते त्याचप्रमाणे हे प्रेमही उत्कट असते. म्हणून येथून जाताना माझ्या मनात जे थोडेसे दुःख सलत आहे ते याच प्रेमामुळे. हे सभागृह अशी एक जागा आहे की जेथे आम्ही वाद केले, मित्र जोडले, चुका केल्या, चांगली कामे केली. इतिहास घडविणारे हे स्थान आहे. समाजजीवन घडविणारी अशी ही जागा आहे. अशा सभागृहातून जाताना विरहाची भावना मनात निर्माण होणे स्वाभाविक आहे. जाता जाता एक गोष्ट सांगणे मला आवश्यक वाटते की, नकळत माझ्याकडून काही चुका झाल्या असतील, कोणाकडे दुर्लक्ष झाले असेल, कोणी दुखावले असतील तर त्या सर्वांची मी माफी मागतो.'

The Speaker, T. S. Bharade (page 127) :

'महाराष्ट्राचे कविवर्य मोरोपंत यांनी म्हटले आहे की, 'झाले बहु, होतील बहु, आहेतही बहु, होतीलही बहु, परंतु यासम हा'. असा हा महापुरुष ! पंडित नेहरूंच्या व्यक्तिमत्वामध्ये अनेक दुर्मिळ गुण होते, अगदी परस्पर विरुद्ध

वाटणाऱ्या गुणांचाही समन्वय त्यांच्या ठिकाणी होता. एकाच व्यक्तिमत्वामध्ये विद्युल्लतेचे चापल्य आणि सागराचे गांभीर्य कोण पाहणार? एकाच व्यक्तिमत्वामध्ये बालकाच्या निष्पापतेचे दर्शन आणि वृद्धाला लाजविणारा पोरकटपणा कोण पाहणार? एकाच व्यक्तिमत्वामध्ये विश्वाचा विचार करणारी चिंतनशीलता आणि क्षणिक अन्यायाविरुद्ध संतापाचा उद्रेक कोणी पाहिला आहे? असे विविधतेचे व्यक्तिमत्व असलेला पुरुष पृथ्वीवर दुसरा झाला नाही. सागराचे गांभीर्य, सूर्याचा प्रताप, चंद्राची शीतलता, गंगेची पवित्रता, हिमालयाची उत्तुंगता व स्वर्गाची दिव्यता या साऱ्या गोष्टी हजारो वर्षांनंतर पंडित नेहरुंच्याच व्यक्तिमत्वात पाहावयास मिळाल्या.'

'हजारो वर्षे मानवाने ज्ञानविज्ञानाच्या आधारे जग बदलण्याच्या कामी प्रभावी यश मिळविले आहे; पण जग बदलण्यास मानव यशस्वी झाला तरी मानव बदलण्यास मानवाला यश आले नाही. परंतु महात्मा गांधी, पंडित नेहरू यांना मानवाला बदलण्यात यश आले कुठल्याही प्रयोगशाळेत विज्ञानाने जे साध्य झाले नाही, राज्यकर्त्यांना जे साध्य झाले नाही, राजकारणधुरिणांना जे साध्य झाले नाही ते महात्मा गांधी व पंडित नेहरू यांनी आपल्या व्यक्तिमत्वाने सिद्ध करून दाखविले.'

'पंतप्रधान अनेक होतील आणि जातील पण इंद्रप्रस्थाचे लोकप्रस्थात रूपांतर करणारा अजातशत्रु युधिष्ठिरासारखा असा पंतप्रधान पुन्हा होणार नाही. भारताला असा पंतप्रधान लाभला हे आपले महाभाग्य होय. ज्याप्रमाणे कमळाचे पान पाण्यात असूनही ते पाण्यापासून अलिप्त राहावे त्याप्रमाणे देशाच्या पंतप्रधानपदासारख्या अत्त्युच्च आसनावर आरुढ झालेले असताना देखील सत्तेच्या चिखलापासून, सत्तेच्या मोहापासून पंडित नेहरू अलिप्त राहिले. जनक राजाप्रमाणे ते सदैव विदेही राहिले. खऱ्याखुऱ्या अर्थाने ते राजर्षी होते. राज्ये चालतील, चालणार आहेत, नेतृत्व चालेल; पण द्रष्टत्व दिसणार नाही. पंडित नेहरूंनी मानवतावादी वृक्षाची मुळे या देशात रुजविण्याचा प्रयत्न केला. अशा युगप्रवर्तक पुरुषाच्या नेतृत्वापासून आज भारत वंचित झालेला आहे. ही उणीव भरून काढणे सर्वांचे काम आहे.

Shrimati Maniben Desai (Nominated):

'He has upheld the prestige of this House as also of the Parliamentary system of democracy. He was very competent, clear in his thoughts and always ready to help the members whenever they were in any difficulty. He provided guidance not only to the Members of the legislature but also to the Minister and he gave his advice impartially without fear or favour to those who approached him.

As I said, he took great pains to enhance the prestige of the Maharashtra Legislature and the prestige of the Maharashtra Branch of the Commonwealth Parliamentary Association. I am not saying this because I am a Maharashtrian, but I have heard legislators from other States saying this.'

Bharatiya Vidya Bhavan

Bhavan's *Biography & Autobiography* Series

BIOGRAPHIES

	Titles	Author
1.	Mahatma Gandhi: His Life & Times	*Louis Fischer*
2.	Rajaji (A Study of his Personality)	*Masti Venkatesa Iyengar*
3.	Mokshagundam Visvesvaraya	*Pandri Nath*
4.	Mahayogi Sri Aurobindo	*R. R. Diwakar*
5.	Living Biographies of Great Philosophers	*Thomas & Thomas*
6.	Living Biographies of Great Religious Leaders	*Thomas & Thomas*
7.	Living Biographies of Great Scientists	*Thomas & Thomas*
8.	Sri Ramakrishna Paramahansa	*R. R. Diwakar*
9.	Minstrels of God Vol. I	*Bankey Behari*
10.	Minstrels of God Vol. II	*Bankey Behari*
11.	Adi Sankara: His life & Times	*T. M. P. Mahadevan*
12.	The Life & Teachings of Saint Ramalingar	*S. P. Annamalai*
13.	In the Steps of the Yogis	*Swami Vijayananda*
14.	Narayana Guru	M. K. Sanoo
15.	A Saint of Modern India	*J. P. Vaswani*
16.	The Rishi	*T. L. Vaswani*
17.	Sadguru Gnanananda	*His Devotees*
18.	Six Illuminates of Modern India	*Dilip Kumar Roy*
19.	Sri Swaminarayan	*M. C. Parekh*
20.	The Blind Leads the Unblind	*Gulabrao Maharaj*

21.	Gulabrao Maharaj	*S. D. Kopardekar*
22.	Baba of Mukteshwardham	*M. D. Chhugani*
23.	Swami Vivekananda: Literary Biography	*Carebanu Cooper*
24.	Munshi- Self Sculptor	*Jayana Sheth*
25.	The Rajaji Story	*Rajmohan Gandhi*
26.	Yogi Krishnaprem	*Dilip Kumar Roy*
27.	Annie Besant	*Sri Prakasa*
28.	My Uncle Netaji	*A. C. Bose*
29.	Mirabai: Her Life & Times	*Herman Goetz*
30.	Life & Times of Sir Pherozeshah Mehta	*V. S. Srinivas Sastri*
31.	Pathway to God Trod by Saint Ramalingar	*G. Vanmikinathan*
32.	R.D. Ranade and His Spiritual Lineage	*V H Date*
33.	Prophet of Indian Nationalism	*Dr. Karan Singh*
34.	Jayashankar Sundari & Abhinayakala	*B. B. Panchotia*
35.	Jagadischandra Bose	*Manoranjan Gupta*
36.	Prafullachandra Ray	*Manoranjan Gupta*
37.	The Indomitable Sardar	*K. L. Panjabi*
38.	Swami Shraddanand	*M. R. Jambunathan*
39.	Ten Saints of India	*T. M. P. Mahadevan*
40.	Swami Ramatirtha	*S. R. Sharma*
41.	Lord Gauranga	*Sisir Kumar Ghose*
42.	The Creed of Saint Vinoba	*Vasant Nargolkar*
43.	Netaji the Man-Reminiscences	*Dilip Kumar Roy*
44.	Swami Shivanand (Sri Mahapurush Maharaj) Reminiscences	*His Devotees*
45.	Pageant of Great Lives I	*Several Contributors*
46	Pageant of Great Lives II	*Several Contributors*
47.	Pageant of Great Lives III	*Several Contributors*
48.	The Life of Joseph Stalin	*Louis Fischer*
49.	Vishva Kavi Rabindranath Tagore (Hindi)	*Illachandra Joshi*
50.	B G Kher: The Gentleman Premier	*M. V. Kamath*
51.	Akbar Vol. I	*J. M. Shelet*
52.	Akbar Vol. II	*J. M. Shelet*

53.	Jawahar Tarangini or Bharat Ratna Shatakam (Sanskrit)	*S. B. Velankar*
54.	Jawahar Jeevanam (Sanskrit)	*S. B. Velankar*
55.	Munshi: His Art and Work, Vol. I	*Eminent Contributors*
56.	Munshi: His Art and Work, Vol. II	*Eminent Contributors*
57.	Munshi: His Art and Work, Vol. III	*Eminent Contributors*
58.	Munshi: His Art and Work, Vol. IV	*Eminent Contributors*
59.	Bhakta Mira	*Bankey Bihari*
60.	Bhagwan Buddha	*R. R. Diwakar*
61.	Sir Asutosh, My Grandfather	*P. K. Banerjee*
62.	Mere Gurudev (Hindi)	*Manjula Trivedi*
63.	Ramanuja's Teachings in His own words	*M. Yamunacharya*
64.	Ramakrishna and Vivekananda	*Dr. Karandikar*
65.	Saints of Maharashtra	*Savitribai Khanolkar*
66.	Saint-Poets of Maharashtra	*N. N. Subramaniam*
67.	Sufis, Mystics and Yogis of India	*Bankey Behari*
68.	Sankara's Teachings in his Own Words	*Swami Atmananda*
69.	Crusaders of the Fourth Estate in India	*Ed. K. Srinivasan*
70.	The Indian Triumvirate	*V. B. Kulkarni*
71.	Sri Ramakrishna Paramahansa	*S. W. Warnekar & R. N. Roy*
72.	Ananthasayanam Ayyangar-A Biography	*S. K. Mangammal Chari*
73.	Bejoy Kumar Sinha: A Revolutionary's Quest for Sacrifice	*Srirajyam Sinha*
74.	Jagadguru Chandrasekharendra Saraswati: Charitra Aani Dharmakarya (Marathi)	*His Devotees*
75.	Mahayogi Gagana Giri	*Ashish*
76.	Fragrant Memories	*Indira Devi*
77.	A Statesman Among Jurists: Biography of Dr. Alladi Krishnaswami	*Alladi Kuppuswami*
78.	The Uncommon Doctor	*D. B. N. Murthy*
79.	Devi Ahalyabai Holkar: The Philosopher Queen	*M. V. Kamath*

80.	Surendranath Dwivedy: Relentless Crusader	*Several Contributors*
81.	History Through Personalities: Footprints, Finger prints, Hand prints on the Sands of Time	P. Ramalingam
82.	Girdharilal Mehta: Sangam of Sree and Saraswati	*Sh. Mammohan Thakur & Shri Kaul*
83.	Conqueror of the Self: G. D. Birla A Study of his Life	*Naresh Jotwani*
84.	The Mahatma and the Poet	*Mrinalini Sarabhai & E. S. Reddy*
85.	Seshadri Swamigal of Tiruvannamalai	*S. A. Subramaniam*
86.	Gandhiji's Leadership: The Oceanic Circle Beyond Time & Geography	*Jana Anand*
87.	Mahatma Gandhi Vazhulkei Varalaru (Tamil)	*Tr. by V.Krishnamachari*
88.	Lokmanya Tilak: In the Temple of Justice	*Shrinivas B. Belvi*
89.	Five Holy Men	*Hemant Bambawale*
90.	Living for Others	*D. B. N. Murthy*
91.	Antar Darshan 'Yek' Satya Anubhuti (Hindi)	*Pushpa Vinod Nemani*
92.	Dr. S. R. Ranganathan (1892-1972) Pragmatic Philosopher of Information Service	*Yogeshwar*
93.	A Love-Story with Reflections on Life and Death	*R. Gopalakrishnan (RGK)*
94.	Madhva's Teachings in His Own Words	*B. N. K. Sarma*
95.	Khasu Subba Rau : Fine Editor and Fearless Journalist	*Dr. D. Amjaneyulu*
96.	Mahatma Gandhi: Man of the Millennium	*Ed. Sheshrao Chavan*
97.	Narayana Guru: The Social Philosopher of Kerala	*Satya Bai Sivadas & P. Prabhakar Rao*
98.	Dr. M. S. Swaminathan: Scientist & Humanist	*Dr. R. D. Iyer*
99.	Loknayak JP: Man of the Century	*Sachchidanand*
100.	The Legacy of Baba Amte	*Veena Adige*

AUTOBIOGRAPHIES

	Titles	Author
1.	Roses in December	*M. C. Chagla*
2.	UNU Saturday's Son	*UNU*
3.	Ganpuley's Memoirs	*N. G. Ganpuley*
4.	Sunset Reflections	*P. S. Tolani*
5.	To the Best of My Memory	*P.B.Gajendragadkar*
6.	Whom Enemies Sheltered	*Maj. R. G. Salvi*
7.	Bird & Cage	*S. N. Bhattacharya*
8.	Many Worlds Revisited	*K. P. S. Menon*
9.	The Sacred Touch	*T. S. Avinashilingam*
10.	Baba Prithvi Singh Azad: The Legendary Crusader	*Baba Prithvi Singh Azad*
11.	Time & Chance	*James Callaghan*
12.	Light of Other Days	*Saraswati Menon*
13.	Life in Greater India	*B. Bissoondoyal*
14.	98 Not Out	*Lord Fenner Brockway*
15.	Towards the Silver Crest of Himalayas	*G. K. Pradhan*
16.	A Philosopher Looks Back	*T M P Mahadevan*
17.	The Path	*Madhuri*
18.	Autumn Leaves	*O. Pulla Reddi*
19.	Adrift on the Ganga	*Satyanarayana Sinha*
20.	The Pen as My Sword	*K. Rama Rao*
21.	Bombay High Court: Half a Century of Reminiscences	*K. M. Munshi*
22.	Cancer Made Me	*Kasturi Sreenivasan*
23.	Jail Diary	*C. Rajagopalachari*
24.	Flight to Soviet Land	*Satyanarayana Sinha*
25.	One Thousand Full Moons	*K. P. S. Menon*
26.	From Literature to Religion	*D. S. Sarma*

27.	On the Wings of Time	*Kamala S. Dongerkery*
28.	Yamaraja's Brother	*Dr. M. K. Mani*
29.	A Journey within the Self	*Deepa Kodikal*
30.	Hand of Destiny Vol. I (The Turning Point)	*C. Subramaniam*
31.	Hand of Destiny Vol.II (Green Revolution)	*C. Subramaniam*
32.	Ten Faces of a Crazy Mind	*K. S. Karanth*
33.	The Stars that Guide	*Dr. K. Damodaran Nambiar*
34.	How God Came into My Life	*Several Contributors*
35.	What Life Has Taught Me	*Several Contributors*
36.	A Movement in Time	*Apa Pant*
37.	Living as a Doctor	*Dr. P. Tirumala Rao*
38.	An Airman's Saga	*Capt. V. Sundaram*
39.	A Cabinet Secretary Thinks Aloud	*B. G. Deshmukh*
40.	A Cabinet Secretary Looks Around	*B. G. Deshmukh*
41.	Twenty-five Years with HMT	*Dr. S. M. Patel*
42.	What Life has Taught Me	*Swami Ranganathananda*
43.	Memories Men and Matters	*N. Raghunathan*
44.	Events Extraordinary	*T. R. Krishnamachari*
45.	Looking Back	*K.Santhanam*
46.	As It Happened!	*Jaisukhlal Hathi*
47.	A Reporter at Large	*M. V. Kamath*
48.	Pilgrims of the Stars	*Dilip Kumar Roy, Indira Devi*
49.	With Malice Towards None	*S. H. Belavadi*
50.	The Journey of a Man of Law	*Justice Dr. B. P. Beri*